PUFFIN BOOKS
MAHATMA GANDHI

Subhadra Sen Gupta has been writing since college and has worked as a copywriter in many advertising agencies. She specializes in historical fiction and non-fiction, travel writing, detective and ghost stories as well as comic strips. She is currently writing the scripts of comics based on the famous Feluda stories available in Puffin.

Other books in the *Puffin Lives* series

MAHATMA

Gandhi

THE FATHER OF
THE NATION

SUBHADRA SEN
GUPTA

PUFFIN BOOKS

PUFFIN BOOKS
Published by the Penguin Group
Penguin Books India Pvt. Ltd, 11 Community Centre, Panchsheel Park,
New Delhi 110 017, India
Penguin Group (USA) Inc., 375 Hudson Street, New York, New York 10014,
USA
Penguin Group (Canada), 90 Eglinton Avenue East, Suite 700, Toronto,
Ontario, M4P 2Y3, Canada (a division of Pearson Penguin Canada Inc.)
Penguin Books Ltd, 80 Strand, London WC2R 0RL, England
Penguin Ireland, 25 St. Stephen's Green, Dublin 2, Ireland (a division of
Penguin Books Ltd)
Penguin Group (Australia), 250 Camberwell Road, Camberwell, Victoria
3124, Australia (a division of Pearson Australia Group Pty Ltd)
Penguin Group (NZ), 67 Apollo Drive, Rosedale, North Shore 0632,
New Zealand (a division of Pearson New Zealand Ltd)
Penguin Group (South Africa) (Pty) Ltd, 24 Sturdee Avenue, Rosebank,
Johannesburg 2196, South Africa

Penguin Books Ltd, Registered Offices: 80 Strand, London WC2R 0RL,
England

First published in Puffin by Penguin Books India 2010

Copyright © Subhadra Sen Gupta 2010

10 9 8 7 6 5 4 3 2 1

ISBN 9780143330813

Typeset in Bembo by Eleven Arts, New Delhi

Printed at Anubha Printers, Noida

Contents

You are called a true Vaishnava,
When you can feel the pain of others.
You do good to others who face misery,
And do not let pride enter your mind.
You tolerate and praise the whole world,
And you do not criticize anyone.
You keep your actions and your thoughts pure,
Your motherland is blessed by you.

Vaishnava jana to tene kahiye je
Peed parayi jaane re
Par dhukkhey, upkar kare tohey
Man abhimaan na janey re
Sakal lok maan sahuney bandey
Nindaa na kare keni re
Vaach kachh man nischal rakhey
Dhan-dhan janani teni re . . .

—Bapu's favourite bhajan,
Vaishnava jana to by Narasingh Mehta

1 🚶 We Call Him Bapu

On his passport he was Mohandas Karamchand Gandhi. The poet Rabindranath Tagore gave him the title 'Mahatma'—the great soul—but he was rather uncomfortable with that. He was amused when the British Prime Minister Winston Churchill described him as a 'half naked faqir'. Nelson Mandela calls him a 'sacred warrior', others describe him as the 'the saint of the spinning wheel' and we now declare him as our 'Father of the Nation'.

However, for the common people of India—that row of women planting rice in a muddy field under a hot sun, or a sweaty cook at a street-side food shop, a teacher in a village school or a weaver at his loom—he remains simply Bapuji, beloved father. And he liked that name.

The man in his chhoti si dhoti

He was a courageous freedom fighter, a very shrewd politician and a passionate social reformer. He was also a man who enjoyed a good joke, loved to walk and led a quiet green movement to protect our environment at a time when no one had even heard of the term. And he disliked putting on his false teeth and ate the most boring food you can imagine.

Mahatma Gandhi was the most unusual leader this country has ever seen.

Cartoonists loved to caricature him because it was so easy to capture his gangly, eccentric looks. He looked like a benign, slightly absent-minded grandfather, until you noticed the large, sharp, intelligent eyes. He had a round domed bald head with big ears that stuck out at an angle, and it was these ears that made Sarojini Naidu call him 'Mickey Mouse', which made him laugh.

He had a stick thin body and long spindly arms and legs that made him look like a human grasshopper. When he was reading anything he would perch round, steel-rimmed glasses at the end of his long, bulbous nose. He was very conscious of time and always wore a battered steel watch, tied at his waist with a string. He had a surprisingly sweet and gentle smile that charmed even the most cynical news reporter.

As he walked along the dusty village paths with his tall bamboo stick, he looked like any Indian villager. This image was at the centre of Gandhiji's ability to win the hearts and minds of his people. He did not wear the suit and tie of a city man or the expensive silk achkan of a maharaja or nawab. Even though people called him a 'mahatma' he was not clad in the saffron robes of a holy man.

He wore the clothes worn by the poorest Indian. At a time when there was no television, Bapu made a visual statement that even an illiterate farm labourer could understand—he was one of them, he understood the trials of their lives and he was on their side. His charisma came from this very human, transparent love for his land and his people.

The world still remembers him

What is amazing is how Mahatma Gandhi remains a part of our lives and continues to inspire people across the world. Great freedom fighters like Martin Luther King of the United States and Nelson Mandela of South Africa have acknowledged that they learnt from Gandhiji's philosophy of satyagraha. We still write books and make films about the man in his *chhoti si dhoti* and coin new words like *gandhigiri*.

In the Gandhi Museum in Delhi, one whole wall is covered with postage stamps featuring his face, printed in just about every country in the world. Roads are named after him and his statue stands in many important cities in every continent. We not only remember the serious and important things he said but also his jokes, because he had a wonderful sense of humour; and unlike most of our leaders, he enjoyed laughing at himself.

So what did Gandhiji do to make a whole nation love him so much that they followed him out into the streets to face the batons of the police and go proudly to jail?

He did not win freedom single-handed—no human being can do that—but he led a great band of freedom fighters in their struggle against the might of the British empire. He created an army of unarmed soldiers who showed the greatest courage of all—they fought with the weapons of peace and non-violence. It is a fascinating story because no one in the history of the world had done that before.

Keeping life simple

Gandhiji never let his popularity go to his head. He was never dictatorial, and persuaded people to his way of thinking through discussions. He also had no problem admitting publicly that he had made a mistake, once calling one of his decisions a 'Himalayan blunder'. He never demanded unquestioning obedience from his followers, who often disagreed with him, and all party decisions were taken after long debates. Tough, hard-headed leaders like Vallabhbhai Patel and Motilal Nehru were not easy to convince, and the Congress Party did not listen to him when he opposed the partition of India.

A deeply religious man, he was also absolutely secular. He opposed the caste system and took off his sacred thread when he discovered that Dalits were not allowed to wear them. He prayed every day but did not perform any religious rituals. He also led many satyagraha campaigns to force temples to open their doors to everyone. At his prayer meetings there were readings from holy books of all religions and they sang both bhajans and hymns. He was inspired not just by the Bhagwad Gita but also Jesus Christ's Sermon on the Mount, the Koran, Jain beliefs on non-violence and the teachings of Lord Buddha. Once when he was asked if he was a Hindu he replied, 'Yes I am. I am also a Christian, a Muslim, a Buddhist and a Jew.'

He was a fascinating mix of highly original ideas and eccentric fads and fancies. He was suspicious of modern medicines and preferred nature cures of mud packs and herbal pills. His diet was so boring that people avoided sitting next to him at meals because he would promptly offer them his bland mash of boiled vegetables cooked without salt, oil or spices and bitter neem chutney that he insisted was great for digestion. His dessert was palm gur that he called 'chocolate', or fried groundnut powder sprinkled on mashed bananas that he called 'butter'!

All his possessions could be packed into a single khadi bag—a few cotton dhotis and chaddars, a pair of battered chappals, his rosary beads, a copy of the Gita and his false teeth that he only put on to eat. Also paper, pen and ink, an enamel bowl and a tin spoon that he took away from Yeravda Prison (after asking the permission of the prison official of course!). He also carried a small towel that he would soak in water and place on top of his bald head when it got too hot.

He slept for about four hours and would get up at three in the morning to read his letters which he often answered personally, scrawling a reply on the back of used envelopes or postcards because he hated to waste anything. He would use pencils until they were such tiny stubs that he could barely hold them; and once when a pencil was misplaced, he made everyone hunt for it till it was found. He talked so much that he decided on a day of silence every week to rest his vocal cords. He was always surrounded by people demanding his attention and often said he quite enjoyed going to prison because then he got some rest. He called Indian jails 'His Majesty's hotels'!

What's so special about him?

Many of his colleagues used to be puzzled by his extraordinary popularity. People would walk for days and then wait patiently under the hot sun for hours just to catch a glimpse of him. Stationmasters at small stations would risk their jobs and halt the train in which he was travelling so that they could offer him flowers and fruits. He could make a whole country come to a halt just by going on a fast. How did he do it, they all wondered. In fact the magic was a simple one—people sensed that he genuinely cared.

Most political leaders think they have to give loud speeches full of angry words as they wave their arms to impress people. In contrast Gandhiji, who was a rather shy man, always spoke in a quiet, logical, reasonable manner as if he was carrying on a conversation with his listeners. However, his gentle, courteous manner did not mean that he could be bullied. His mild exterior hid a will of iron; he was not afraid of pain and he had a sharp, perceptive mind that his opponents learnt to respect.

India's freedom was the first brick to fall from the edifice of imperialism and soon it all came tumbling down as colonized countries in Asia and Africa became independent. Later, satyagraha inspired Martin Luther King's battle for civil rights in the United States and Nelson Mandela's freedom march in South Africa, proving once again that satyagraha and non-violence are relevant even today and that they work. In tribute the United Nations General Assembly now observes Gandhiji's birthday, 2 October, as International Day of Non-violence.

Saint, half naked faqir, shrewd politician, social reformer, party boss—he was all that and more. This is the story of how he led one of the most unusual freedom struggles in the world—one that mobilized unarmed, peaceful people, and not fighters with guns, and no one had ever done that before!

For Gandhiji, life was an endless search for that ever elusive truth. It was India's good fortune that he took us along on that tumultuous journey and taught us that freedom begins the moment we refuse to be afraid.

Bapu and children
We have all seen photographs of Mahatma Gandhi with children. There is a delightful one of a laughing Bapu rubbing noses with a baby in his arms, and another one of a little boy leading him by holding one end of his walking stick and Bapu following obediently.

For the children growing up in Sabarmati Ashram he was a benign grandfatherly figure, who was a friend and playmate. He was their 'Bapu' (father) and Kasturba was 'Ba' (mother). He called them his Vanar Sena, his monkey army, and took them swimming in the river, taught them to peel potatoes in the kitchen and spin cotton thread on charkhas. They would even have contests to see who could spin the most cotton in which Bapu and Kasturba would join in. In one such contest they both lost to one of their granddaughters.

An American social worker Horace Alexander, who visited Sabarmati Ashram in 1928, noticed how the children constantly surrounded Bapu and how patient he was with them. As he wrote, 'After a rest, I went to evening prayers. When all were assembled, he came walking quickly and sat down in the centre and the chanting began. When the prayers were over, each member of the ashram gave his or her report on the amount of spinning done. This lasted fifteen or twenty minutes and was rather tedious. I noticed that the children ran playfully around the Mahatma while this went on and he thrust out his hand as if to catch them as they ran past. Some years later, one of the children, now a grown-up man, told me how difficult he had found it, as he grew up, to realize that the kind old man, so simple and friendly, of his childhood days, was the same as the Mahatma.'

While travelling to Britain by ship in 1931 to attend the Round Table Conference, Gandhiji spent most of his time spinning and reading on the deck as children surrounded him, clamouring for his attention. In London he stayed at the East End, a poor locality, and was soon 'Uncle Gandhi' to the neighbourhood children. Once, as he was walking past, one small boy yelled, 'Hey Gandhi, where's your trousers?' making the Mahatma laugh heartily. He was in London on his birthday and the children presented him with two woolly dogs, three pink birthday candles, a tin plate, a blue pencil and some jelly sweets, and he took them all back with him to India.

Surprisingly, he was a very strict and demanding father to his four sons while they were growing up in South Africa. Once when his son Manilal visited Sabarmati, he immediately noticed how indulgent his father was towards the children in the ashram. The episode is described in Gandhiji's biography by Louis Fischer. Manilal said, 'Bapu you have vastly changed from the time we were under you. You never pampered us; I remember how you made us do laundry work and chop wood; how you made us take the pick and shovel in the bitterly cold mornings and dig in the garden, to cook and to walk miles.' Gandhiji did not deny the truth in his words, laughed and said, 'Well children, are you listening to what Manilal is saying?' and he went on indulging them.

Many of the youngsters at the ashram joined the freedom struggle, including Vitthal Thakkar, who at sixteen was the youngest marcher to Dandi. Gandhiji did think kids were smart and that adults should listen to them. As he said, 'The greatest lessons in life, if we would but stop and humble ourselves, we would learn not from the grown-up learned men, but from the so-called ignorant children.'

2 🏹 A Boy from Porbandar

1869–1892

In the latter half of the nineteenth century Porbandar was a sleepy little coastal town on the Arabian Sea in Gujarat, in a region called Kathiawar. In the 1860s India was a part of the British empire and Queen Victoria was the Empress of India. A large part of the country was administered directly by the British government in India, but there were also princely states ruled by rajas and nawabs who owed their loyalty to the British Crown. Among them were huge Indian princely states like Hyderabad and Jaipur, and also tiny principalities like Porbandar and Rajkot.

Porbandar must have been a beautiful coastal town and one wonders if the young Gandhi ever spent time on the beach watching the waves flow across the sands. In his writings, the ever practical Mahatma never bothered to wax lyrical about his home town. Many years later his English disciple Charles Freer Andrews visited Porbandar and wrote that the town 'becomes a vision of glory at sunrise and sunset when the slanting rays beat upon it, turning its turrets and pinnacles into gold'.

The family Gandhi

The prime minister to the Raja of Porbandar was called a dewan, and in the 1860s it was a man named Karamchand Gandhi, who was called 'Kaba' by everyone. He lived in a small, double-storied, whitewashed house with his fourth wife Putlibai (his earlier wives had all died) and his large joint family of brothers and cousins. They belonged to the caste of Modh Banias, a trader community. Kaba and Putlibai's youngest child was born on 2 October 1869 and named Mohandas. He was the fourth child of the fourth wife and had two brothers and an older sister. His full name was Mohandas Karamchand Gandhi, but the family affectionately called him 'Moniya'.

Two photographs of Kaba and Putlibai have survived. Kaba Gandhi sits wearing an achkan and pyjama and has a very regal white moustache drooping over his lips. Putlibai stands holding a string of prayer beads and has soft eyes and a gentle, slightly vulnerable face. In his autobiography, *My Experiments with Truth,* Gandhiji writes that his father had no formal education but was an experienced manager and administrator—'he had no education save that of experience'. He was a religious man who visited temples and read the Bhagwad Gita, but the family was not orthodox about religion. Kaba had a temper, and young Mohandas was a bit nervous of him.

Young Gandhi was closest to his mother and writes about her, 'The outstanding impression my mother has left on my memory is that of saintliness.' She was gentle and generous, and cared for everyone in the family with equal love and kindness. She was the first to get up in the morning and worked late into the night. Her loving nature left a deep impression on the quiet, shy boy who spent most of his time trailing her around the house instead of playing with other children. One day he would show the same kindness and empathy for everyone—humans, animals and birds. At the ashram in Sabarmati, Gandhiji would not only worry about the people, but also the goats and cows living there.

A very ordinary boy

In his very honestly written memoirs, Gandhiji admits that he was a very ordinary boy—shy, timid and not very good in studies. For many years he needed a light in his room at night because he was scared of the dark, ghosts and snakes. In school he found it difficult to memorize the multiplication tables and comments frankly, 'My intellect must have been sluggish and my memory raw.' He was so shy that after school he would head straight for home instead of spending time with friends.

When Mohandas was seven, Kaba Gandhi became the dewan of the state of Rajkot, and his family moved with him. Mohandas completed his schooling there. A photograph of a seven-year-old Mohandas has survived, taken at Porbandar. He is sitting in a high-backed chair, his right hand resting on a table beside him. He is wearing a dhoti, a high-necked jacket and an embroidered cap. There is an expensive-looking necklace around his neck and a dot of bindi on his forehead. He sits looking solemnly at the camera, with large eyes under arched eyebrows—a gentle, oddly vulnerable face, and you get a feeling he did not enjoy the experience of being photographed; at least he did not smile.

There was one incident in school that revealed the future man. A British inspector arrived at their class and the boys were given five English words to spell. The teacher noticed that Mohandas had spelled the word 'kettle' wrong and he quietly signalled that Mohandas should copy the correct spelling from the slate of the boy sitting next to him. Mohandas refused and was later scolded for being stupid. He would display this firm honesty all his life. Gradually he improved in studies and even won prizes in school. He writes that he loved geometry and Sanskrit because he found them logical and easy to understand. However, he was not athletic; he hated gymnastics and cricket, though he did play with his top, balloons and spun his stick after a wooden peg playing gilli danda.

Young Mohandas does not sound like a future national leader, does he? Compare a boy who hides behind his mother and forgets his multiplication tables and in his own words is a 'mediocre student' with the towering leader who led a freedom struggle, where lakhs of people became his devoted followers. Gandhiji's life proves just how much each of us is capable of achieving if we only have the courage and the determination to do so. As Gandhiji's biographer Krishna Kripalani says, 'He was not born a genius and did not exhibit in early life any extraordinary faculty that is not shared by the common run of men . . . If there is anything extraordinary about him as a child it was his shyness, a handicap from which he suffered for a long time.'

One day this painfully shy man would gather his courage, take a shaky breath and face a phalanx of police armed with sticks and guns; he would address giant public meetings, facing a sea of watching faces, and calmly walk into the King of England's Buckingham Palace, his chappals slapping on the marble stairs. You can do so much if you have the courage to follow your dreams and not be defeated by the failures that you will always face on the way.

Of myths and legends

Like all children Mohandas loved to listen to stories about gods and goddesses, demons and celestial dancers from Hindu mythology and especially from the Ramayana and the Mahabharata, but surprisingly he was not impressed by hero-warriors like Arjuna or Lord Krishna. Among the characters he admired were Raja Harishchandra, who always spoke the truth; Shravana, who died while caring for his aged parents; and Prahlad, who defied his demon-father because of his love of Lord Vishnu. All of them suffered because of their faith in truth, and in many ways they are examples of satyagraha that Gandhiji would one day propagate. His satyagraha was a fight for truth led by peaceful soldiers ready to face every obstacle with courage.

The Gandhi family was very liberal in its religious beliefs. They were Vaishnavas, worshippers of Lord Vishnu, but also visited Shiva and Jain temples. Mohandas' nurse Rambha taught him to chant the *Ramanama*, saying that it would stop him from being afraid, and he chanted Lord Rama's name till the day he died. Kaba Gandhi had Muslim and Parsi friends who were invited to his home for religious discussions. Putlibai often asked a Jain monk for advice. Even as a child Mohandas did not like the 'glitter and pomp' of temples and later stopped going to them, but all his life he remained curious about religion and read deeply about all of them.

Kasturbai Makhanji

When Mohandas was thirteen he was married to Kasturbai Makhanji, the daughter of a Porbandar businessman. Kasturbai, who was later called Kasturba or just 'Ba', was a few months older than him. For the boy marriage meant a lot of new clothes and presents, days of celebrations and a new companion whom he could bully. However, his bossiness did not work too well because his child bride had a will of her own and often refused to obey him. What made it worse was that she was not scared of ghosts or snakes! Kasturba was illiterate, and her husband's attempts to teach her to read and write were not too successful; she just wasn't interested and finally she only learnt a basic Gujarati. Looking back to those years Gandhiji said that child marriage was a 'cruel custom' and always opposed it. Mohandas and Kasturba would be married for sixty-two years.

In his teens, Mohandas fell into bad company and

even learnt to smoke and drink in the company of a spoilt rich man's son called Sheikh Mehtab, who found an ingenious reason for his bad habits. He convinced the shy, scared Mohandas that the British were able to rule India because they ate meat. So it was their 'patriotic' duty to eat meat in order to become strong and force the British to leave. Mohandas, belonging to an orthodox vegetarian family, was reluctant until Mehtab told him he was also not afraid of snakes. So the boy went off to taste the forbidden food, hated the taste and was sick all night. He was tormented by nightmares in which 'a live goat was bleating inside me'. He persisted in his 'patriotic duty' for a while longer, but finally gave it up in relief.

Mohandas was sixteen when Kaba Gandhi fell seriously ill. The boy cared for him with great devotion but at the time when he died, the son was not there and he deeply regretted it. After completing his schooling Mohandas joined a local college in Bhavnagar, but he did not like it there. At that time the family decided that he should study law in England and then try for the post of a dewan. Mohandas was keener to study medicine, but obeyed the wishes of the family elders. Initially Putlibai was reluctant to let her son go, but Mohandas was very eager. He finally convinced her by taking a solemn vow in front of a Jain monk that while in England he would not touch wine, women or meat.

Mohandas and his older brother arrived in Bombay for his journey to England and faced a new challenge. A council of elders of the Modh Bania community declared that it was against their religion to cross the seas. At that time there was a superstition among Hindus that you became polluted and lost your caste if you travelled overseas. Once again young Gandhi showed great resolution and refused to obey the diktat; at which he was excommunicated from his caste. This meant that other Modh Bania families would not let him enter their homes or do any business with him.

On 4 September 1888, Mohandas sailed from Bombay for Southampton, England. He was eighteen and already the father of a son.

The first voyage

A painfully shy, inarticulate young man, all alone on a ship going to a strange land, he must have been petrified. On the long voyage he mostly stayed in his room and even ate there, much too nervous to face the crowds in the dining hall and the challenge of that intimidating row of shining cutlery beside his dinner plate. He had brought fruits and sweets with him, and just ate that for a while.

He was miserable, homesick and hungry for the first few days in London, as he writes, 'I would continually think of my home and country . . . Everything was strange—the people, their ways and even their dwellings. I was a complete novice in the matter of English etiquette and continually had to be on my guard. There was the additional inconvenience of the vegetarian vow. Even the dishes I could eat were tasteless and insipid.'

He was often hungry because he could only eat some of the dishes that his landlady provided, until to his great relief he discovered a vegetarian restaurant on Farringdon Street. Here he also found a book on vegetarianism that he read carefully and now became a vegetarian by choice. Young Gandhi also went through a phase of becoming a complete sahib, bought suits, fancy hats and ties and spent a long time combing his hair and knotting his tie before the mirror. He took ballroom dancing, violin, French and elocution lessons until he began to feel guilty about spending so much money and decided to concentrate on his studies.

He always kept a meticulous account of all his expenses on food, clothing, postage, bus fare, newspaper and books—three guineas on ballroom dancing, ten pounds on an evening dress from Bond Street. This habit would continue when he was the leader of the Congress Party and kept track of every rupee that was spent. He also began to save on bus fare by walking eight to ten miles every day from college and back. Later his padyatras were his way of connecting with the people as he trudged through villages and towns to listen to people

Dr S. Sinha, who was also a student in London at that time, remembers the sahib Gandhi and it is hard to match this image with the Gandhiji we are all familiar with. Sinha writes that he wore 'a high silk top hat burnished bright, a stiff and starched collar, a rather flashy tie displaying all the colours of the rainbow, under which there was a fine striped silk shirt. He wore as his outer clothes a morning coat, a double-breasted waistcoat, and dark striped trousers to match, and not only patent-leather shoes but spats over them. He also carried leather gloves and a silver mounted stick.' This vision of English elegance would one day wear just a khadi dhoti and chaddar!

The Vegetarian Society

Mohandas joined the Vegetarian Society and his number of friends grew. Among them was a member of the Theosophical Society that was into the exploration of Eastern religions, and he introduced Mohandas to an English translation of the Bhagwad Gita. He was delighted with it, and the Gita would become his companion for the rest of his life. He also read of the life of the Buddha and the Prophet Muhammad. When he read the Bible, the Old Testament bored him, but he enjoyed the life and teachings of Jesus Christ in the New Testament and was deeply impressed by the Sermon on the Mount that he said 'went straight to my heart'.

So for three years his days were spent at the Inner Temple studying law, and the evenings with the members of the Vegetarian Society. Eventually he was elected to its Executive Committee and showed a real talent at organizing events. However, his shyness was still a problem; at least on three occasions he stood up to speak, lost his voice and someone else had to read out his lecture. He could never go beyond the first sentence, 'and only succeeded in making myself ridiculous'. There is a hazy photograph of the Vegetarian Society taken in 1890 and he is clearly the youngest member, sitting in a corner and looking quite happy with life.

Gandhiji, who had a talent for finding a positive side to everything, later said that there was an advantage to his shyness. 'My hesitancy in speech, which was once an annoyance, is now a pleasure. Its greatest benefit has been that it has taught me the economy of words. I have naturally formed the habit of restraining my thoughts. And I can now give myself the certificate that a thoughtless word hardly ever escapes my tongue or pen.'

At this time one of our greatest nationalist leaders Dadabhai Naoroji was working in London. His home became a refuge for the young Indian students there, and among them were Mohammad Ali Jinnah, who would later head the Muslim League, and Mohandas Gandhi, a shy young Gujarati law student, who would one day fight Jinnah's attempt to divide India. There was also the fiery Bhikaji Cama, who was Naoroji's secretary and the first woman freedom fighter of India. She designed one of the earliest national flags. Gandhiji never forgot Naoroji's kindness and wrote later, 'Indeed, he was in the place of a father to every one of the Indian students . . . And so Dadabhai became a real "dada" to me.'

Gandhiji also began to travel, visiting the Great Exhibition in Paris in 1890 where he liked the churches, but was unimpressed by the Eiffel Tower that he called a 'trinket'. In 1891 he was called to the Bar, that meant now he was a qualified barrister, and three days later he sailed for India. A great sadness waited for him at home:

his mother had died and fearing it would affect him badly, the family had not informed him.

Back in India

Mohandas was now the head of a household and for a while tried to introduce Western ways, with oatmeal porridge for breakfast and the drinking of tea and cocoa. He forced everyone to go on long walks, spent a lot of time arguing with Kasturba and had very little money. He began to practise law in Rajkot, but did not get many cases. So he went to Bombay, and here during his first day in court an attack of his dreaded shyness was so crippling that he had to hand over the case to another lawyer. The family must have become very worried about the son from whom everyone had such high expectations.

Even his attempts to introduce himself to the royal court at Rajkot were a failure. His older brother sent him to meet the British Resident at the court. Residents were British officials who were placed in the princely states. They were powerful men as they had a lot of influence over the king and often interfered in the business of the state. Gandhiji's brother hoped that the officer would treat a barrister with respect. Instead, the Resident ordered his peon to make his visitor leave his office. It was Gandhiji's first experience of the arrogance of colonial power and he never forgot it. He hated the atmosphere of intrigue and sycophancy in the royal court and dreamed of escaping.

Mohandas was making a precarious living drafting legal notices and applications, when he got an offer of a legal assignment in South Africa and immediately took it. He had to go and fight a legal case there for a Muslim firm and would be away for a year. He would be paid 105 pounds, first-class fare and all expenses. So in 1893, M.K. Gandhi, bar-at-law, not a very successful lawyer at Rajkot, and the father of two sons, sailed for Durban, South Africa. The ship would travel from Bombay to Durban via Zanzibar, Mozambique and Natal. When he finally returned to India in 1914, twenty-one years later, he was welcomed at the Bombay docks by a crowd cheering a famous fighter against imperialism, apartheid and the colonial might of the British empire.

How South Africa transformed young Mohandas into Mahatma Gandhi is a truly fascinating story.

Bapu's food fads

Everyone found Bapu's eccentric diet fascinating. He grew up in a vegetarian household but his interest in a vegetarian diet began in England when he found the book *A Plea for Vegetarianism* by Henry Salt at a vegetarian restaurant. He read it carefully and had soon joined the Vegetarian Society where they spent all their time discussing whether eggs or milk were allowed in a pure vegetarian diet. Pretty soon he had convinced himself that food that was cooked without spices or salt was the best for health. He began by eating boiled spinach with no spices, then for a while gave up all starch or lived on just bread and fruit. When he gave up eggs it meant no cakes or puddings either. He began to cook for himself and was very proud of his tasty carrot soup.

Later in South Africa he moved one step further and gave up cow's milk, but once when he was seriously ill he agreed to take goat's milk, though he wasn't happy about it. This meant that later in India, during the freedom movement, wherever he travelled his team had to organize a goat. When he was in Yeravda Jail the prison warden had a couple of goats brought in for his famous prisoner. Then in 1931 when he travelled to London for the Round Table Conference, they got off the ship in France and travelled by train. To the horror of the police, an enthusiastic devotee arrived at the Paris railway station with a white goat for Bapu and had to be stopped at the gate.

Sarojini Naidu wrote about her first sight of Bapu and mentions what he was eating. She saw 'an open door framing a living picture of a little man with shaven head, sitting on the floor on a black prison blanket and eating a messy meal of squashed tomatoes and olive oil out of a wooden bowl.'

What did Bapu eat during an average day? His day began with a glass of lukewarm water and honey. Lunch was rotis with vegetables (cooked without spices or salt), lemons, goat's milk and a bitter chutney of neem leaves and garlic. He did start eating some salt and a little ghee after a while and enjoyed taking fruits and lemons. Among fruits he preferred oranges, apples, grapes, raisins and dates. As mentioned, he added fried groundnut powder on squashed bananas and called it butter. His dessert was usually a chunk of palm gur that he declared was as good as chocolate. He never drank tea or coffee but liked curd or cottage cheese made out of goat's milk and a variety of nuts like walnuts and almonds. The rule was that he would eat a maximum of five different kinds of food every day.

Once at Sabarmati Ashram he tried to live exclusively on raw food. Bapu always had a very logical explanation for what he did and here the idea was that if we ate more raw food it would free women from the drudgery of the kitchen and it would also make travelling simpler. The daunting diet that he created included wheat sprouts, groundnut paste, spinach, raisins, lemons, honey and coconut milk. Some brave members of the ashram also joined him, but after a few days they all became very weak, began to suffer from dysentery and colitis and finally, to Kasturba's relief, the experiment was abandoned.

We may call him a food faddist, but he called himself a 'food missionary', making it clear his experiments were not just fads. According to him he was trying to create a balanced, nutritious diet at the lowest possible cost that poor people could survive on. However, he did admit that his personal diet wasn't exactly cheap and he often apologized for that.

Bapu's biographer Louis Fischer describes a communal meal at Sevagram in Wardha where after the recitation of a prayer he was served a 'vegetable stew' with spinach and squash, some salt and slices of lemons, a dab of butter, three tiny boiled potatoes, one boiled onion, roti, papad and a glass of milk. He was the only one in the dining hall who was allowed to use a spoon. At the third such meal he rebelled at another serving of the bland stew and firmly refused Bapu's offer of a second helping. If he was offered the neem and garlic chutney, Fischer does not mention it.

3 🚶 The 'Coolie' Barrister

1893–1914

When Mohandas Gandhi stepped off the ship at Durban, he looked a typical Indian lawyer, clad in a neat frock coat, pressed trousers, polished shoes and a turban. He was received at the port by his client Dada Abdullah Sheth, one of the most successful Indian businessmen in South Africa. Gandhiji was to fight a legal case for him against another Indian trading company. By everyone's calculations the case would take about a year, and that is how long the ambitious young barrister planned to stay. In fact, Gandhiji remained in South Africa for nearly twenty years.

An apartheid world

During his stay in England, Gandhiji had not faced much overt racism; he had lived as a paying guest with an English family and had easily made British friends. It was in South Africa that he first encountered a world where society was divided by the colour of one's skin. Here racism had the sanction of the government and it was an official policy called apartheid. South Africa had been colonized by Europeans, just like India, and its society included Europeans, Africans and Indians. Even though a majority of the people were Africans, it was the white-skinned people who ruled the country. Gandhiji was familiar with the social prejudices based on caste in India, but what he faced now was a society openly full of prejudice and violence against the non-whites.

In South Africa dark-skinned people had no rights—they could not travel about freely or own property, they could not go out after 9 p.m. at night, they were not allowed to enter many places like hotels and shops and Gandhiji was even pushed violently off a pavement. The Indian population consisted of labourers who worked in the coffee and sugar cane plantations. They were poor, lower caste people who had come from India hoping for a better life. The rest were traders like Dada Sheth, who had slowly built up their businesses, and some were very rich and even owned ships. However, they were still second-class citizens who had no rights, and faced constant harassment from white officials who were jealous of their success. They were taxed heavily and not allowed to trade freely.

The whites contemptuously called the Indians 'coolie' or 'sami', and in the official records Indians were referred to as 'semi barbarous Asiatics'. As for the condition of the Africans, it was even worse. Most of them survived as labourers or poor farmers, who never got an opportunity to be educated, could not hope for better jobs like the whites and were like slaves in their own land. They had no way to protest because the laws and the police were against them.

Gandhiji had to go to Pretoria for the case, and during the journey he got a first-hand experience of apartheid. He was travelling in the first-class compartment of a train when at Pieter Maritzburg station a white passenger entered, took one look at Gandhiji and called the train guard. The railway officials insisted that Gandhiji should move to the third-class compartment. When he protested, he was pushed out on to the platform, his luggage thrown out after him, and the train steamed out of the station.

A deeply shaken Gandhiji spent the night in the waiting room, feeling cold and miserable. His overcoat was in his suitcase which was in the stationmaster's office, and fearing more insults he did not ask for it. Shivering and sleepless, he sat up all night and brooded about what had happened to him. Somewhere a seed of determination was planted in the mind of this gentle, peace-loving man—he had to find a way to fight this terrible and unfair system. And his experiences of the following days would completely change his attitude to life. He not only got a true taste of colonialism, but also a sense of what the Dalits faced in India.

Many years later he was asked what was the most creative moment in his life and he recalled that traumatic night at the Pieter Maritzburg station. As Gandhiji's biographer, the historian B.R. Nanda, writes, 'Something happened to him in that bleak windswept waiting-room of Maritzburg railway station . . . from that hour, he refused to accept injustice as a part of the natural or unnatural order in South Africa.'

Gandhiji's troubles were not over yet. He took a stagecoach to Johannesburg and the white conductor forced him to sit outside with the driver while he himself sat inside. Then he wanted to smoke and ordered Gandhiji to travel on the footboard while he took the seat. Gandhiji refused to move, at which the man began to hit him, but Gandhiji hung on to his seat and did not hit back. Finally the other passengers protested and he was allowed inside the coach. Then at Johannesburg he was turned away from the good hotels and finally found a room in a guesthouse run by an African. Even here he was allowed to eat in the dining room only after the white guests said they had no objection.

When they heard about it, Dada Sheth and his friends, all prosperous traders, were not surprised and narrated similar humiliating experiences. Gandhiji could not understand why they never protested, and soon called a meeting of the Indian community in Pretoria, most of whom were Muslim merchants like Sheth. Although most of them were rich, they were not well educated. At the meeting, as anger burnt away his shyness, Gndhiji spoke with confidence and he later said that it was his first successful speech. He said that they should form an association to look after the welfare of Indians, and offered his legal services. This was the beginning of the organization that came to be called the Natal Indian Congress.

Meanwhile, the case he had come to fight was sorted out amicably as he convinced both sides to compromise. His job done, he came back to Durban to catch a ship home. At his farewell party he learned that the government was planning a bill by which Indians were to lose their right to vote. Everyone begged that he delay his departure for a month and help them prepare a petition against the bill, and he agreed.

The petition was presented to the government, but the bill was still passed. The next strategy was to collect signatures for an even bigger petition that would be sent to the government in England. Working feverishly, they collected 10,000 signatures in just a fortnight. This caught the attention of the press both in India and England, and all the reports mentioned the great work done by Gandhiji. For the first time he became a public personality. He later wrote, 'Thus God laid the foundation of my life in South Africa and sowed the seed of the fight for national self-respect.' He would stay in the public eye for the rest of his life.

Gandhiji now decided to stay on for a while longer and so had himself admitted as an advocate in the Supreme Court. Earlier he had been thrown out of a court for refusing to take off his turban, but he now decided to obey the dress code. He was now choosing which battles were worth fighting for and said, '. . . the very insistence on truth has taught me to appreciate the beauty of compromise. I saw in later life this spirit was an essential part of satyagraha.' The Natal Indian Congress was officially established and he became its energetic secretary and showed great skill in organization. This was great training for the time when he would manage the mammoth Congress Party of India.

While he was busy with his political activities, Gandhiji was also fighting for the rights of the poor. His first case was for an indentured labourer named

Balasundaram. These men were called 'indentured' because when they arrived in South Africa they had to sign a contract with a plantation owner. As most of them were illiterate, they did not realize that they could not leave their job until the period of the contract was over, and thus became virtual slaves. When their contract was over they would often try to stay on but the government, wanting them to leave, taxed them so heavily that they could not survive. At times these 'free' Indians were taxed half their yearly earnings.

Balasundaram had been beaten brutally by his white employer and Gandhiji presented proof of this before the magistrate. The employer was summoned to court and found guilty, but instead of demanding that the man be punished, Gandhiji asked that Balasundaram be freed from his contract. The Natal Congress now took up the case of the labourers, fighting to get the taxes abolished and also for better working conditions. Soon labourers were pouring into Gandhiji's office begging for help, and he became so popular that the whites began calling him the 'coolie barrister'. After an energetic campaign he managed to get the tax reduced, but he was not entirely happy with the result.

Back in India

Gandhiji had already been in South Africa for three years and clearly there was much more work to be done. Moreover, as his legal practice was going well he decided to go to India and get his family. It was also an opportunity to tell Indians about how their compatriots were being treated in South Africa and build up public opinion against apartheid among Indians.

Gandhiji arrived in India in 1896 and immediately contacted the press and began giving interviews. He also wrote a pamphlet and distributed it wherever he went. He decided to send some by post, and got all the children in the locality to help him with writing the address and licking stamps. Interestingly, two of his small assistants would one day become his followers. Right from the start he recognized the power of the press and would use it to spread his message to people. Pretty soon the story of the oppression of apartheid was picked up by newspapers in both India and England. It did not make him very popular in South Africa, though.

While he was home in Rajkot there was a plague epidemic and Gandhiji, ever the master organizer, immediately gathered together a team that went from house to house checking their cleanliness. They taught people to keep their toilets clean, and he commented that the poor kept them cleaner than the rich. This campaign to make people aware of the importance of hygiene would become a second nature with him. He was always a social reformer first and then a leader. During the freedom struggle he would talk of the importance of good hygiene, eating nutritious food and wearing khadi as much as the fight for freedom.

Next Gandhiji decided on a long journey to learn about his fellow Indians—a Bharat yatra—travelling in third-class train compartments. It was a journey of discovery as he learnt how ordinary people lived, their problems, hopes and dreams. He also met many nationalist leaders like Surendranath Banerjea, Bal Gangadhar Tilak and Gopal Krishna Gokhale, and everywhere he spoke about the conditions faced by Indians in South Africa.

In Bombay, Pherozeshah Mehta called a special meeting of the Indian National Congress where Gandhiji was the main speaker. As he mounted the stage, the dreaded shyness attacked again, he lost his voice and Dinshaw Wacha had to read out his speech! Among all the leaders, he built the closest friendship with the wise and cultured Gokhale, who was one of the leaders of the Congress Party. Gandhiji was still unfamiliar with the political scene in India and Gokhale became both a guide and a political mentor. One day Gokhale would travel to South Africa to spend some time with his favourite shishya.

Return to Natal

Gandhiji, Kasturba and their two sons Harilal and Manilal sailed for Durban in 1893. Meanwhile, his speeches and writings in India against apartheid had been reported in South Africa and led to much criticism in the press. The whites of Natal now decided that they would not allow Gandhiji to come back to South Africa. First the ship was held at the port and quarantined because the officials said that the passengers may be carrying the plague from India. When after twenty-three days the ship was allowed to dock, an angry crowd was waiting for Gandhiji. Some people suggested that he should leave under the cover of darkness, but he refused to do that.

Next morning he first let Kasturba and the boys leave and then calmly left the ship, planning to walk the two miles to his friend's home. A jeering crowd soon surrounded him and began to punch and kick him until he was down on the ground, badly injured. He would have died if Mrs Alexander, the wife of the police superintendent, had not seen him and rushed to protect him till the police arrived. However, the danger was not over. He took shelter in the home of his friend Rustomji, and the mob followed and surrounded the house.

The police arrived but found it difficult to control the crowd that was getting more and more unruly. Inside, Gandhiji became worried as there were women and children in the house. He decided to leave alone and the police dressed him in the uniform of an Indian constable, tying a metal saucer under the turban to protect his head. In this disguise, accompanied by a detective dressed as an Indian merchant, he quietly slipped out through the crowd. They jumped over fences, squeezed between rails and passing through a store were soon safely inside a police station. Meanwhile, the goons were told that Gandhiji had escaped, but some men refused to believe that he had walked past them and even went inside the house to check.

To everyone's surprise Gandhiji refused to press charges against the men who nearly killed him. He also gave a press interview to explain his activities in India. He wrote later, 'This interview and my refusal to prosecute the assailants produced such a profound impression that the Europeans of Durban were ashamed of their conduct.' For him, making people think again about their behaviour and regret what they had done was more important than getting revenge. He was very good at making people feel guilty about their wrong actions. What we would now call *gandhigiri*!

Gandhiji was fighting for equal rights for Indians as theoretically all subjects of the British empire were equal, but in fact the white subjects were always given preference. He was still loyal to the Crown, always hoping that the government would listen to reason. In 1899 a war broke out between the two white settlers in the region—the English and the Dutch, who were called the Afrikaners. This was the Boer War and Gandhiji organized a group of Indian volunteers to form an Ambulance Corps that would tend to the wounded, often risking their lives to enter the battlefield. After the war ended, he was awarded a medal for his services.

Gandhiji had hoped that their loyalty would be rewarded with Indians getting equal status as citizens of a British colony, but his hopes were soon dashed. As a matter of fact, conditions became worse and soon his faith in the goodness and fair play of the government began to be frayed.

A battle for equality

In 1901 Gandhiji returned to India and even set up a law practice in Bombay, but he was called back to South Africa by his friends. The Indians were facing newer challenges there. He set up a law office in Johannesburg and his practice flourished. The Gandhis now lived in a big house and he could have continued with this comfortable life quite easily. However, he had other dreams. Somewhere the vow he had taken at Pieter Maritzburg station was yet to be fulfilled. He was still thinking about the political status of Indians and started a weekly magazine called *Indian Opinion* to make people more politically conscious.

The government now decided that all Indians had to be registered and their fingerprints were to be taken, as if they were criminals. Of course this law did not apply to the whites. There was a storm of protest and Gandhiji even led a delegation to England, but the law was still passed in 1907. Gandhiji and his followers led a protest march in South Africa and were arrested. A settlement followed with General Smuts, a minister in the South African government, by which a compromise was agreed upon. According to this, Indians would voluntarily register if the Act was repealed, but Smuts did not keep his word and the Act was passed. At this some Pathans became so angry with Gandhiji that they attacked him and he was badly injured.

Now a full scale satyagraha was launched where thousands of registration cards were burnt and then they marched into the district of Transvaal defying a ban order, and hundreds were arrested. Many of the protesters, including Gandhiji, were jailed. During the trial Gandhiji pleaded guilty as he was determined to go to prison. However, witnesses were needed to prove his guilt and so his friends Herman Kallenbach and Henry Polak obligingly stood up and gave evidence against him. This was his first jail term and he later wrote about the terrible conditions in prison where he was kept in a dark cell and made to dig stones, and his followers were starved and whipped. Finally, because of protests in the press, they were released and Gandhiji sent Smuts a pair of sandals that he had made in prison as a goodbye present!

Soon there was a furore among Indians over a new law that only recognized Christian marriages; this meant that all other marriages were illegal. This time the satyagraha was even more widespread, with mine workers and labourers going on strike and even women joining the protests. They faced the police who were armed with batons, some protesters were killed and Gandhiji was jailed again. He was released only after the Indian and British press began to carry reports critical of the South African government. And the law was finally repealed.

By now the loyal subject of the Crown had had enough. At a meeting to mourn the dead, Gandhiji declared that he no longer felt any loyalty towards the British Crown. He was always conscious of the image he presented to the world and he shed his Western clothes to put on the clothes of a satyagrahi. The photograph taken at that time shows a thin, balding man in a long kurta, dhoti and chappals, standing straight, holding a stick and looking rather grimly at the camera.

Satyagraha and ahimsa

During this time Gandhiji had also made a radical change in his lifestyle. He set up two communes that we in India would call ashrams, first the Phoenix Settlement near Durban and then the Tolstoy Farm closer to Johannesburg. Here they lived a very simple, environment-friendly life. They built their homes, grew their own food and lived without any divisions of caste or religion. He 'studied the art' of doing his laundry, became an amateur barber and taught himself all the work of running a farm. He baked bread, made marmalade and something he calls 'caramel coffee', made leather sandals and learnt carpentry. He walked everywhere, and when he had to go to Johannesburg to fight a case he would walk twenty-one miles in a day. It was excellent training for the Mahatma who walked all across India.

His greatest supporters at this rather eccentric experiment were two Europeans: Herman Kallenbach, a wealthy Johannesburg architect, and Henry Polak, a journalist. It was Kallenbach who bought the land for the Tolstoy Farm. Another good friend was his secretary Sonya Schlesin. Polak and Kallenbach may have worked happily in the farm, but it was not an easy change for everyone. Kasturba, who was a traditional woman, found it hard to give up the comforts of her home in the city, and when she was asked to clean the toilets she had a huge fight with her husband.

This was the time when Gandhiji gradually evolved the philosophy that he called satyagraha and his faith in ahimsa. Simply explained, satyagraha means our faith in the truth; it has also been described as 'soul force' or 'truth force' and 'militant non-violence'. What he was saying was that we had a right to fight all forms of oppression but we had to fight peacefully—through ahimsa or non-violence. This meant in simple terms that if you had to protest against any unfair action by the government you led a peaceful protest march, not a violent one.

Gandhiji must have had a tough time explaining this rather unique idea to his followers. Everyone believed that to win freedom you had to pick up a gun and start a revolution. After all, that is how the French and American Revolutions had succeeded. As many of his critics asked, why should a government listen to peaceful marchers? They would just send out the police and the army to beat you down. Gandhiji explained that satyagraha was the cleverest way for an unarmed and powerless people to defeat a powerful oppressor.

It is a very subtle idea, as the British discovered later in India. How do you fight a people who march out with flags, singing songs, rows and rows of not just men but also women and children? They do not retaliate at your lathi charge, they do not hit back. When they are beaten to the ground they just pick themselves up and march on. The more the police attack the more people join the satyagraha till the whole country is out on the streets and the jails are overflowing with prisoners. Satyagraha makes it impossible for a government to function as the country comes to a halt.

Now remember, Britain had colonized India to make

money. Colonization was business; it was about making profits by exploiting a country, and if the country was paralysed it became very costly to run it. The factories are shut, no one is paying taxes, offices, law courts, schools and colleges are closed. At the same time the newspapers are full of pictures of unarmed people being beaten by policemen riding on horses and carrying thick sticks with metal tips, and reports of innocent people dying. The whole world sits up and protests and makes the government feel highly embarrassed. Satyagraha is a moral war. Many years later in the United States when Martin Luther King led his satyagraha for equal rights for African Americans, the pictures of the police attacking peaceful protesters with dogs had the same effect.

The British had always spread the myth that they had colonized Asia and Africa for the good of the people. The great white races were civilizing these barbarian people, educating and modernizing their societies. It was what they called 'the white man's burden', and the odd thing is that they were talking of saving countries like India and China whose civilizations were much older than theirs! Now the world began to ask, if the colonized people were so happy being subjects of the British Crown what were they doing dying on the streets singing of freedom? Was this the real image of the 'benevolent' British empire?

Satyagraha was peaceful but it was not the way of the coward. Gandhiji made it very clear that ahimsa needed more courage and determination than any other form of protest. To stay peaceful and not get provoked into hitting back was much harder than answering a bullet with another bullet, because a violent battle is one that never ends. Violence only leads to greater violence but what do you do against an opponent who does not hit back? Also, as it is a path everyone can take, there are more satyagrahis to take the place of the one who has been jailed or killed. Satyagrahis are stubborn people and they refuse to give up.

As he kept saying, satyagraha needs lots of courage and even more patience, but it is the best weapon for the poor against the rich and powerful. When a whole nation stands up and protests then even the most brutal and dictatorial government will ultimately be forced to retreat. Years later, another great satyagrahi would take South Africa to freedom—Nelson Mandela, who finally defeated apartheid. He has always acknowledged that he learnt much from the teachings of Gandhiji and calls him a 'sacred warrior'. Satyagraha is real people power.

His work done in South Africa, Gandhiji was now ready for a much greater challenge in India. The First Satyagrahi was now ready to challenge the greatest colonial empire in the world.

Kasturba

Everyone called her 'Ba' and she was quite a personality. Kasturbai Makhanji was born on 11 April 1869, the daughter of a Porbandar businessman Gokuldas Makhanji. She was married to Mohandas Gandhi when they were both thirteen, and through a tumultuous life spent in South Africa and India they were together for sixty-two years.

Few women see the upheavals that Kasturba handled during her lifetime. From the quiet little town of Porbandar she was transported to South Africa and then catapulted into the hurly-burly of our freedom struggle, and she took all this with amazing courage and fortitude. The changes she saw were often drastic; for example she was leading a life of ease in a mansion in Johannesburg and suddenly her eccentric husband decided to shift to a farm. At Phoenix Farm she discovered she had to cook and wash and even clean toilets because Gandhiji wanted to try simple living. She was furious.

Soon they were in the middle of a satyagraha and Kasturba was gathering her courage and leading a protest march of women and going to jail. Within a few years Gandhiji had brought them all back to India and had plunged into the freedom movement. They were now rattling around the country in dirty, hot and crowded train compartments. They were mobbed everywhere they went, and for the rest of her life she lived in the public eye with very little privacy. As he was often away, she was left to cope alone with her family at Sabarmati Ashram.

Kasturba was a traditional Hindu wife, but never obedient or docile. Gandhiji had to work hard to convince her and was a bit nervous of her quick temper. When they were married young, Mohandas tried to boss his wife, insisting that she take permission before going out to play, but she ignored him. It wasn't easy living with a husband who was always experimenting with family life.

For instance, on his return from England he insisted that they lead a Westernized life, with everyone eating with knives and forks and wearing shoes and stockings. She and her sons rebelled especially at the stockings that were hot to wear and made their feet stink. Then suddenly they became traditional Hindus again and were living in an ashram and spinning thread on a charkha!

Gandhiji's insistence on simple living and high thinking meant Kasturba had to make many sacrifices. When they were leaving South Africa, the Indian community gave them many gifts and he decided that they would not accept any. The gifts were to be sold and the money given to charity. Kasturba, who had set her heart on a necklace, was furious and he had a tough time convincing her that he was right.

Gandhiji's constant experiments with food caused her endless problems. One day he was living just on nuts, next he had stopped taking salt and then on another he vowed to give up drinking cow's milk. Once he became seriously ill and the doctors wanted him to drink milk but the stubborn Mahatma refused. Everyone was at their wits' end until Kasturba finally managed to convince him to drink goat's milk which he did for the rest of his life.

Gandhiji was quite dictatorial at home with his own theories about medicine, food and the bringing up of children. He insisted on educating his four sons, Harilal, Manilal, Ramdas and Devdas, at home and made them live a spartan life without any luxuries. Harilal rebelled and he had a rather tumultuous relationship with his father, often publicly opposing Gandhiji. This caused a lot of heartache to Kasturba. When Harilal's wife died, she brought up his four children at Sabarmati Ashram.

She had been brought up as a traditional Hindu and in those days the belief in untouchability was deeply ingrained in people's mind. So when Gandhiji brought a Dalit couple to stay at Sabarmati, both Kasturba and Gandhiji's nephew Maganlal rebelled and she nearly left the ashram. It took a lot of persuasion to make her change her mind. Unlike the rest of the world she was not always impressed by her saintly husband and often calmly ignored his diktats. Gandhiji told his biographer Louis Fischer, 'Ba takes tea in spite of the fact that she lives with me. She also takes coffee. I would even lovingly prepare it for her.'

When she was married Kasturba was illiterate, and even though Gandhiji tried hard to teach her, she wasn't interested in studying and just learnt to read and write a basic Gujarati, her mother tongue. He was still trying to educate her in 1943 when they were both imprisoned in the Aga Khan Palace in Poona. He was teaching her geography and to everyone's amusement she kept mixing up the names of places. At that time they were both seventy-four years old.

Gandhiji used to tell the children at Sabarmati that he was scared of her. Once when unexpected guests arrived in the afternoon, lunch was over and Kasturba had gone off for her nap. Gandhiji and a few boys crept into the kitchen, where he told them to prepare some food but to do it very quietly so that she did not wake up. Then he quickly left. But someone dropped a brass thali, which woke up Kasturba and she demanded why she had not been called. If Bapu thought he would escape her ire he was mistaken, because he got a scolding in public in the middle of his prayer meeting.

It wasn't easy being married to a saint who was also a freedom fighter. Right from South Africa she lived in fear that Gandhiji would be killed. Quite a few times he was seriously injured and there were also the long fasts that made him seriously ill. If you study her photographs, the young Kasturba is a beautiful woman with large eyes and a delicate, fine-boned face, but soon the face begins to reflect the hardships she endured. In many of the photographs we see her sitting slightly behind her husband, calm, stoic and loving. As Fischer, who met her often, says of her, 'Being herself and being at the same time a shadow of the Mahatma made her a remarkable woman.'

In 1942 when Gandhiji was arrested during the Quit India Movement she threatened to give public speeches unless she was allowed to join him and they were imprisoned together in the Aga Khan Palace. Here her chronic bronchitis worsened and even though Gandhiji nursed her tenderly, she died on 22 February 1944. Gandhiji was devastated and took a long time to recover from the loss of his lifelong companion. His follower Mira Behn wrote, 'With Ba it was as if a part of Bapu departed.'

4 🚶 Discovering the Real India

1914–1919

Gandhiji returned to India in January 1915 with his family. His exploits in South Africa had made him quite well known in cities, but across the vast landscape of his homeland he was quite unknown. Members of the Congress Party were keen to meet him and wanted him to become involved in politics. Gandhiji's mentor Gokhale, however, did not agree. As he commented astutely, Gandhiji knew South Africa better than he did his own country; he had left as a young man and had been away for two decades. So his suggestion was that Gandhiji should first learn about his country and he should 'keep his ears open and his mouth shut'. Gandhiji obeyed, for a while, but then it was always hard to keep him quiet for very long.

So Gandhiji and Kasturba now began a marathon journey across the land, always travelling by third-class compartments in trains. He clearly enjoyed the experience as it was a great way to get in touch with people in the noisy, crowded, dirty train bogies swaying across the countryside, but Kasturba did not find it very easy. As soon as the news of his travels spread, excited crowds began to wait for him at railway stations to load him with flowers. This was the beginning of a life spent forever under public scrutiny, constant demands for attention by people and endless hard work. And he would cheerfully follow a punishing schedule of eighteen–hour days for the rest of his life.

A poet and a Mahatma

Gandhiji and Kasturba went to Shantinikentan, an experimental school opened by the poet Rabindranath Tagore. In many ways Shantiniketan echoed the spirit of Gandhiji's Tolstoy Farm. Here students attended classes under the leafy shade of banyan and mango trees, and with the usual subjects they also learnt Indian classical music and dance, painting and sculpture. Shantiniketan went back to the spirit of ancient Indian ashrams where education was given within nature and was about expanding your knowledge and imagination and not about examinations.

The poet and the First Satyagrahi became instant friends. Gandhiji called Tagore 'Gurudev' and Tagore dubbed him as the 'Mahatma' or great soul, and both the names stuck. Gandhiji was never very comfortable with the title and once commented wryly, 'the woes of Mahatmas are known to Mahatmas alone.' Always energetic about spreading all his pet theories about food, he tried to introduce a vegetarian diet in the school kitchen and made the teachers and students do all the cooking as the cooks were very unhygienic. Tagore indulgently let him do so. Of course the moment he left, the cooks returned and the Bengali menu went back to fish curry and rice. B.R. Nanda tells another interesting story: 'One day Gandhi told him (Tagore) that to fry in ghee or oil was to turn bread into poison. The Poet replied solemnly, "it must be a very slow poison. I have been eating puris the whole life and it has not done me any harm so far"!'

Though the two men did not meet very often, they wrote regularly to each other and remained close friends till Tagore's death in 1940. In many ways they were very different in character and often disagreed about politics, but when it came to the matter of India's freedom, Tagore was a passionate supporter of Gandhiji's satyagraha. As Fischer says, they were 'sentimentally inseparable, soul mates to the end, they waged verbal battles, for they were different.' One of Gandhiji's most favourite songs was Tagore's *Ekla chalo*, which says that if no one listens to your call then you walk alone. If your cause is right, but no one will talk to you and turn their heads away in fear, you speak out alone. This song captures the very essence of Gandhiji's life because so many times he started alone and only very slowly others understood what he was trying to do and followed him.

Soon after he arrived at Shantiniketan, Gandhiji got the news that Gokhale had died and he cut short his travels to attend Gokhale's funeral. He finally settled in Ahmedabad where he set up an ashram by the banks of the river Sabarmati. He and his followers planned to concentrate on social work, and decided that members of all caste and religion would live in the ashram together.

The ashram was made up of red-tiled roof huts nestled among trees, a cowshed, a kitchen garden and a pond. They lived a very simple life, growing their own food, tending to the cows and goats, spinning and weaving khadi on charkhas and doing community service in nearby villages. Sabarmati was Gandhiji's anchor, where he would retreat to revive his spirits after the tumultuous events of the freedom struggle.

Going to Champaran

In 1916, when Gandhiji attended the Congress session at Lucknow, he was still not sure if he would join politics or just concentrate on social service. Starting an experimental satyagraha was very far from his mind. At Lucknow, a farmer named Raj Kumar Shukla from Champaran in Bihar came up to him begging that he come and help the indigo farmers there. Gandhiji had never heard of Champaran and knew little about the problems of indigo farmers, and so was not very keen to go. The persistent Shukla followed him to Sabarmati and extracted a promise that on his next trip to Calcutta he would visit Champaran. A few months later, when Gandhiji got off the train at Howrah station, there was a smiling Shukla waiting for him on the platform! When they arrived in Patna, Shukla took him to the house of a local lawyer, Rajendra Prasad, but the lawyer was away. They stayed the night there but the servants refused to let Gandhiji take water from the well as they did not know his caste!

One day Rajendra Prasad would become the first President of India.

Arriving in Champaran, Gandhiji learnt of the terrible lives of indigo farmers and how they were exploited by their European landlords. Indigo was a dye for cloth and there was a big market for it in Europe, so the farmers were forced to grow indigo instead of food crops. They were paid very little, and if they refused the landlords sent their men to beat up the peasants, take away their land and burn their homes. The police, who were in league with the landlords, did nothing to help.

Crowds of peasants gathered to see the man who had come to listen to them, and he was taken to one village riding on an elephant like a raja. The landlords immediately complained to the magistrate, who ordered Gandhiji to leave the district. He refused and was arrested. When he was brought to the court at Motihari, a huge crowd of farmers gathered threateningly outside, making the magistrate very nervous. To everyone's amusement the magistrate sent Gandhiji out to calm the crowd and Gandhiji obligingly did so! Then to make matters worse for the poor man, he admitted his guilt and requested that he be given the maximum punishment. The magistrate imposed a small fine, but Gandhiji said that he would not pay as he had no money. At this the exhausted man just let him go.

Gandhiji, always a meticulous man, wanted to discover for himself exactly what the problem was and so he walked from village to village talking to people.

He was surprised to discover that he was the first Congress leader to have visited the area, and realized how out of touch the party was with most of the country. The party members were all Western educated men, who met in cities to give long-winded lectures in English about constitutional rights and education. However, they had no idea of the reality of the villages. One day, Gandhiji would open the doors of the party to the peasants and factory workers, the weavers and potters, and transform the Congress into a real people's party.

In his typical, precise, well-organized way he collected the facts from 8,000 farmers. As he sat in the village chaupals he also spoke to them about better hygiene, eating nutritious food and the importance of getting their children educated. Kasturba had joined him, and as they walked through village after village they were shocked at the utter poverty of the people who often did not even have a second set of clothes, lived in tiny earthen huts and just had one meal a day. Later when a commission was set up by the government, Gandhiji went as the representative of the farmers, and faced with his mountain of facts the commission had no option but to pass an order in favour of the farmers.

The landowners were ordered to pay back some of the money they had taken from the farmers, who were now free to grow whatever crop they wanted. Soon an artificial indigo dye was developed in Europe; indigo farming died out in Champaran and the landlords all left. What was much more important was that Gandhiji taught these poor, powerless people not to be afraid any more, but to unite and speak up for their rights in case of injustice. Gandhiji said about Champaran, 'What I did was a very ordinary thing. I declared that the British could not order me about in my own country.' It was in Champaran that Gandhiji gathered his first batch of devoted followers—J.B. Kripalani, Mazharul Haq, Rajendra Prasad and Mahadev Desai; the latter would become his secretary and constant companion for twenty-six years.

Ahmedabad and Kheda

The news of a single man taking on the government spread like wildfire and made Gandhiji a national figure. He was the first leader to realize that the cause of the farmers was most important when most Indians lived in villages; without it no freedom struggle could succeed. Soon peasants and factory workers were begging him to lead their protests. The most urgent appeal came from the workers at the textile mills of Ahmedabad.

As always Gandhiji carefully studied the situation and decided that the workers' demands for better pay and working conditions were valid. He decided that the workers could go on strike after they promised to remain peaceful and not hold any violent demonstrations. The mill owners refused to discuss their demands and as the strike dragged on and on, energies began to flag. The workers feared starvation, and hearing this, on an impulse, Gandhiji announced that he would go on a fast to show his sympathy. This was his first fast, and one day he would turn this into a powerful way to make the whole country listen to him. After three days the mill owners gave in because they were afraid of putting the life of a mahatma in danger.

Next Gandhiji answered the call of the farmers of Kheda in Gujarat. They were facing a drought, but the local administration insisted that they pay all their taxes in full. Gandhiji suggested a satyagraha of paying no taxes in which even the richer farmers joined. After four months the government changed its mind and the taxes were reduced. This was the satyagraha where Gandhiji was helped by Sardar Vallabhbhai Patel, a rich and successful lawyer who gave up his practice to join the freedom movement and was one of the greatest leaders of the Congress. A man who used to wear natty suits and played bridge at an exclusive club now wore khadi and stayed in the huts of peasants at Kheda as he plotted a no-tax campaign.

The Rowlatt Act

The First World War started in 1914 and the Congress supported the government in the hope that India would gain some form of self-government after the war was over. What they wanted was Dominion Status like the white colonies of Australia, South Africa and Canada. In these countries the people ran their own government even though they remained a part of the British empire. When the war ended, the government passed the

Montagu–Chelmsford Act and it was a great disappointment: real power remained firmly in the hands of the viceroy and the governor of the provinces.

Then the Rowlatt Act was passed supposedly to check the revolutionaries who often attacked unpopular British officials. It in fact took away all civil rights from the people and gave unlimited powers to the police as people could now be arrested without warrants and imprisoned without a trial for as long as the police wanted. The whole country erupted in protest and Gandhiji moved centre stage with his first nationwide satyagraha. At that time he was staying in Madras with his friend C. Rajagopalachari and brooding about how they should protest. He said later that he got his idea in a dream. It was going to be a hartal. 6 April 1919 was declared Satyagraha Day to be observed as a day of mourning. People would stay home, fast and pray; schools, colleges and shops would remain shut and peaceful protest marches would be taken out.

This was the first time the Congress had organized such a huge protest across the country, and unfortunately it did not stay peaceful. Later Gandhiji, who was always quick to admit a mistake, said he had made a 'Himalayan blunder' in thinking that people would obey him. His mistake was that he did not realize that people had to be trained in satyagraha. The most violent protests took place in Amritsar where two Englishmen were killed and a woman missionary was injured. The army was called in on 12 April 1919 and the military commander Brigadier

General Reginald Dyer issued an order banning all public gatherings in the city. Unfortunately most people did not hear about it and it led to a disaster that changed our history.

Jallianwala Bagh

Next day, 13 April, was Baisakhi, the new year in Punjab. It was the day when people from the villages around Amritsar came to the city to celebrate a new harvest. They prayed at the Golden Temple and then spent the day visiting fairs and gardens. Many of them ended up at a park called Jallianwala Bagh. It was a small, walled space with only one proper entrance. Here a holiday crowd had gathered, unaware of General Dyer's ban order. It was a peaceful crowd that included women and children. In one corner a man was reciting poetry and giving patriotic speeches.

Dyer marched in at the head of fifty Gurkha soldiers, blocked the only gate as soldiers took up positions as if they were facing a violent mob. He gave no warning, nor did he ask the people to leave; he just ordered the soldiers to fire. As the garden was surrounded by a high wall the people had no escape route and over a thousand people were killed and many more injured. The soldiers kept on firing for ten minutes, with Dyer pointing to the places where the crowd was the thickest. Then leaving behind a scene of utter carnage he marched his men out again. No effort was made to help the injured people who were left to die. For the rest of his life Dyer never exhibited the slightest remorse for his action.

Dyer was certain that after this massacre the British empire would be safe for the next hundred years. What he, in fact, did was to wake up the Indians and make them question the rule of the British. For over a century they had been fed with the pill of the benevolent and beneficial rule of the Raj and how it cared for Indians. Now as India watched in horror, Dyer was not punished but was only asked to resign from the army. He was welcomed as a hero in England, the House of Lords praised him and newspapers hailed him as the 'Saviour of Punjab' and the 'Defender of the Empire'. One paper started a public collection in his name and money poured in.

In India there were widespread protests. Tagore returned his knighthood in utter disgust, writing in anguish of the 'insults and sufferings undergone by my brothers' that has been 'ignored by our rulers'. The agony of Punjab continued as it faced terrible police brutalities, with people made to crawl on the streets and being flogged in public. And this hurt the Punjabis even more because thousands of Sikh soldiers had died in Europe during the World War fighting for Britain.

After Jallianwala Bagh India was no longer interested in small drips of reluctantly given political rights; they only wanted swaraj—complete freedom. And Gandhiji's soul force satyagarha was the weapon that the nation chose to use in this highly unequal battle between a poor and unarmed nation and the mightiest imperial power in the world.

Gandhiji and the Congress

To lead any campaign across a nation as vast as India, a political party needs funds, great organizational skills and a leader who can get complete discipline from his followers. The Congress Party now turned to Gandhiji and he gradually took over the leadership of the party and made some crucial changes in its organization. He created a truly national and secular party.

The first thing he did was open the doors of the party to everyone. As the membership fee was kept low, people from small towns and villages poured in. He travelled relentlessly addressing rallies, inviting people to join, and made people aware of their rights. This would be continued by his younger followers like Jawaharlal Nehru and Sardar Patel, who taught people about democracy so that by the time we held the first elections in independent India, we had an electorate that though poor and illiterate was politically aware, understood democracy and knew its rights.

Gandhiji was a genius at organization, a meticulous maker of lists and a master at raising funds. The nationwide campaigns were organized by a flood of postcards giving precise instructions. Nothing escaped his attention. During the Congress sessions he would worry about everything, from the availability of clean drinking water to cleanliness and the seating arrangements. He sent off party workers to canvas for members in the districts and soon there were Congress flags flying in small towns and even villages. This network of party workers held the country together during the chaotic days after the partition of India.

The image of the Congress as a gathering of English-speaking city men was now completely changed. Soon local party meetings were being held in regional languages, and national gatherings were in Hindustani. The members were often khadi-wearing social workers and young enthusiastic men, who were willing to work in villages. Now everyone—from a rich lawyer in Calcutta to a metal worker in Moradabad, a farmer in Madhopur to a weaver in Kanchipuram—were all Congresswallas and freedom fighters. The Indian National Congress had become a truly national party.

Trouble in Sabarmati

Gandhiji had no money and the Sabarmati Ashram ran on donations from people. Once the ashram got into serious trouble when Gandhiji brought a Dalit couple and their young daughter to live there. Dudabhai was a teacher from Bombay, and he arrived with his wife Danibehn and daughter Lakshmi.

In those days prejudices about caste were so deep that in the beginning the ashram people refused to let Danibehn enter the kitchen or share a room with the family. When Gandhiji insisted that everyone live together like one family, many ashram inmates left. Even his nephew Maganlal and wife Kasturba had to be persuaded to stay. Then as the news spread, donations that mostly came from the rich businessmen of Ahmedabad began to dry up. Soon his secretary Mahadev Desai told him that they had enough money for just one more month and Gandhiji was at his wits' end wondering how he would keep the ashram going.

Then one day a young man drove up to the ashram gate in an expensive car and without saying a word he handed Gandhiji a bag of money and drove off. Later he discovered that this was Ambalal Sarabhai, a mill owner, and he had donated thirteen thousand rupees, which was a huge amount at that time. Soon the ashram was on its feet again and many of his followers came back.

A few years later, Gandhiji led a strike by the workers of the textile mills at Ahmedabad. They wanted better pay and ultimately the mill owners had to agree to their demands after Gandhiji went on a fast. The biggest mill owner was Ambalal and when Gandhiji was standing at the gates of his mill giving long speeches, right there next to him, raising angry slogans, was Ambalal's sister Anasuya Sarabhai!

5 🚶 India Refuses to Cooperate

1920–1928

Right after the Jallianwala Bagh massacre many observers noticed a radical change in the attitude of Indians to the British Raj. It became clear that Indians had begun to lose their faith in the British empire. This was really rather surprising, because after being a colony for over a century most people had become quite reconciled to their state and felt that being ruled by the supposedly benign and caring British empire was a good thing. As a matter of fact they could not even imagine an India without the British running it.

The British were supposed to be the 'mai baap sarkar', a government that ruled like a kind parent who cared and protected its brown-skinned subjects. It was a feeling that was subtly encouraged by the government right from school where textbooks started with a lesson about the wonderful British government. Behind this feeling of obedience and loyalty was a deep sense of inferiority as we felt we were not good enough to rule ourselves. So in 1919 most Indians, including many leaders of the Congress, believed that India was still not ready for independence and that the country would collapse into chaos if the British left.

Jallianwala changed all that. Indians had always had great faith in the justice and fair play of the government, but here was General Dyer mercilessly shooting down innocent, unarmed people, even women and children, at a peaceful gathering and he was not punished for his utterly inhumane act. Instead he was moving scot-free and was rewarded by the public in Britain. Even worse, this mishap happened in Punjab, where young men had joined the British army during the World War and thousands had died on the battlefield defending the British empire. The government had made many promises of giving self-government to India once the war was over and many leaders, including Gandhiji, had believed them. Sadly, the Montagu–Chelmford Act of 1919 gave little and the Rowlatt Act took away whatever little rights Indians had, including their civil rights against arrests and searches by the police and even the right to a speedy trial.

Indians felt betrayed and angry and what made it worse was that daily life had become very difficult for them after the war. Prices were very high, salaries were low, there were few jobs, workers in factories were going on strike everywhere and then the monsoon failed and farmers faced a drought. Finally, even the poorest and most loyal among Indians came to the sad conclusion that their sarkar did not really care for them. They were here to be exploited for the benefit of the British people. Indians finally understood that they were a colonized people in an unequal world, where a white-skinned person would always be favoured against a brown one.

General Dyer had claimed arrogantly that his actions would end all rebellions forever, but Jallianwala had the opposite effect. Indians lost their faith in the Raj and suddenly freedom was worth fighting for.

It was at this crucial juncture that Gandhiji stepped forward with a plan for a nationwide movement aimed at gaining freedom, and he called it a satyagraha through non-cooperation. The idea ignited a spark in the minds of Indians and made them finally break through the shackles of blind loyalty, fear and inferiority, and step out in thousands to follow a man they now revered as a mahatma, a great soul. The Non-cooperation Movement of 1920–22 did not bring swaraj as Gandhiji had optimistically promised, but it united the country and made us a nation. When one reads history books, from this juncture one senses that freedom was indeed possible and we could win it.

Who is this Gandhi?

Gandhiji's appearance on the public stage and the storm of popularity that swept the country astonished the British and even puzzled many of his colleagues in the Congress. Even a modern-day Bollywood film star cannot match the clamour of adoration that he handled every day for the rest of his life. Gandhiji's popularity can be gauged by this conversation between two British officials. Sir Thomas Jones, secretary to the British cabinet, asked, 'How many of the three hundred and ten million in India has heard of Gandhi?' Dr Mann, Director of

Agriculture, Bombay replied, 'Three hundred and nine million!'

He had an unusual charisma and the ability to charm and convince the most doubtful people. For example, in the beginning, leaders like C.R. Das and Lala Lajpat Rai were sceptical of his plans, but within a few months they were at the head of protest marches in Bengal and Punjab. He combined this with a genius for organization, was a master at collecting funds and could work harder than any other leader. He was a shrewd judge of men, and built up his own team with talented men and women like Jawaharlal Nehru, Sardar Patel, Maulana Azad, Sarojini Naidu, C. Rajagopalachari, Rajendra Prasad and J.B. Kripalani, who carried out his programme.

During the non-cooperation campaign, when he travelled across India spreading the message of satyagraha, the train would be stopped at stations by people who sat on the tracks and refused to move. At other places the railway staff risked their jobs and stopped the train. People waited for hours and hundreds would fall to their knees when they saw him. People loaded him with fruits and flowers as sadhus reached in through the compartment window and dropped their rudraksha beads on his lap. At times when the train chugged into a station late at night, Gandhiji would be woken up to go out and say a few sleepy words. From now till his death twenty-eight years later, he would always be surrounded by people clamouring for his attention and would at times retreat to his ashram at Sabarmati through sheer exhaustion. He used to joke that he quite liked going to prison because then he had some peace and quiet to do some thinking!

This gentle, courteous and rather reserved man, talking in his soft, reasonable voice, was actually saying some rather dangerous things that made many Congress leaders very nervous. He was saying, we'll break the law but we will do it peacefully. We will refuse to buy British goods, burn their mill-made cloth, refuse to go to school, college or government jobs, quit the army and the police but no one will pick up a gun or even a stick against the police.

No one had come up with plans for such an ambitious, nationwide campaign before, and the Congress leaders had some genuine worries. How could a small political organization like the Congress manage such a huge campaign in a country the size of India? Also, there was the ever present danger of violence and they remembered how Punjab had burned while protesting against the Rowlatt Act. Satyagraha would need a lot of planning, organization and a large, disciplined team that could spread out to cities, towns and villages and lead the campaign; and they doubted that the Congress had the manpower to do all this. Most of them missed the point that a freedom movement can only succeed when the whole country takes part in it.

Also, many people found the theory of satyagraha hard to understand. They all thought a fight for freedom meant you picked up guns and bombs, started a revolution and fought a war of independence. Instead, it was to be a satyagraha of non-violent, non-cooperation and how would that work? It was in fact going to be a very polite revolutionary uprising, and no one had ever heard of that before! The American civil rights leader Martin Luther King, who followed many of Gandhiji's strategies of non-violent protests, said of satyagraha, 'Christ gave us the goals and Mahatma Gandhi the tactics.'

Over the years many historians have tried to analyse the reasons behind Gandhiji's astonishing popularity. You must remember, this was a time without radio, television, or the Internet. The only medium of news was newspapers, and very few people could read. It seemed as if the news of the Mahatma spread like magic through the air and for the poor he became a religious icon. He was their 'Gandhi Maharaj', who would fight the British and bring them freedom so that their miserable lives could get better. He was also their father, their beloved Bapuji, and he did look the part in his dhoti and chaddar that was so different from the natty suits and expensive achkans of the other Congress leaders.

No leader before him and none after possessed such an ability to read the public mind, and while the Congress was still shying away from a nationwide agitation, he knew that the country was ready for satyagraha. His connection to people was extraordinary. He was different, he spoke the people's language, he listened to them, he was sympathetic and he was one of them. It was, as B.R. Nanda says, a 'sudden, almost elemental impact of his personality on the imagination of his countrymen.'

Something many of our political leaders forget is that people are not stupid. They listen and they judge, and they sensed quickly that Gandhiji was a man who was not after either power or wealth. As a matter of fact, he was not even trying to win popularity. He was there to serve the people as he cared deeply about everyone— not just the rich industrialist or zamindar, but also the potter, the weaver, the Dalit leather worker, the housewife in purdah and the teenager dreaming of going to school. I can only think of one other modern leader who has possessed these rare qualities of generosity, empathy and simple humanity with an absence of personal ambition— Nelson Mandela. He also never hankered for power, happily dancing with his people in one of his jazzy, brightly-coloured shirts. Look carefully at their photos: Gandhiji and Mandela have very similar smiles—joyous, full of humour and open to the world. Great men are often simple men because they care.

So it was the right time, the right leader and the right plan. In spite of his surging popularity if you think Gandhiji found it easy to convince the Congress to start the Non-cooperation Movement, you'll be mistaken. There was strong opposition from most of the leaders and it took detailed proposals and many persuasive speeches to carry the motion. He was often heckled at the meetings and many of the leaders walked out in protest, but Gandhiji never gave up. As a matter of fact in the beginning the only senior leader to support him was Motilal Nehru and that was more because his son, a young, passionate Jawaharlal, was completely bowled over by Gandhiji.

In 1920 the senior leaders were all full of doubt at Gandhiji's ambitious plans, but the common members and the younger leaders were all for it. To resolve the issue a special session was called in Calcutta on 4 September where they would vote on the plan. Speakers like Bipan Chandra Pal, Annie Besant, Madan Mohan Malaviya and Mohammad Ali Jinnah spoke against the motion. Gandhiji's reply was logical and passionate, and as Nanda says, 'in less than half an hour he demolished the case of his opponents. He refuted the charge that his programme was impracticable; even though he had no more than six week's experience of non-cooperation behind him.' Even his critics in the press like Natarajan, the editor of *Indian Social Reformer*, had to acknowledge his 'splendid courage'. The resolution was passed by a narrow majority of 148 votes for and 133 against.

By the time the annual Congress session was held at Nagpur three months later, the mood had changed and a majority of the members were ready for the agitation. They wanted it to be led by Gandhiji and the leaders, sensing the popular feeling, gave in. Here Jinnah, still stubbornly opposed to the plan, stood up to speak and the audience booed him off the podium. A very proud man, he walked out of the hall, left Nagpur, resigned from the Congress Party and would soon become the president for life of the Muslim League. Jinnah had at one time been the rising star of the Congress, and he never forgave Gandhiji for usurping his place. Nagpur was the turning point for the Congress, and most party leaders sensed the change in the air. As the historian B.R. Nanda says, 'Henceforth he could do without the Congress, but the Congress could not do without him.'

What did non-cooperation mean?

Now what did non-cooperation really mean? And what did the people have to do? Like most of Gandhiji's ideas it was simple and effective but also at times delightfully vague. He was like an engineer who was always tinkering with his satyagraha machine and at times even changing his mind. Basically the idea was easy: Indians had to stand up and say very politely and very, very peacefully, 'No. Thank you!'

It was to be a war without violence. The people would make it impossible for the British to run the government. Students were to walk out of schools and colleges; government servants, members of the army and police were to quit their jobs; banks would stay closed; factory workers were to walk away from their machines; lawyers would boycott the courts and shops were to down their shutters. Simply, they were going to bring the country to a halt and do it peacefully. This was the time when some of the most successful lawyers of the country like C.R. Das, Motilal Nehru, C. Rajagopalachari, Saifuddin Kichlew and Vallabhbhai Patel gave up their law practices, put on khadi and began to live the simple life of a satyagrahi. Then everyone returned all titles and honours given by the government, and Gandhiji gave back the Kaiser-i-Hind medal that he got for organizing an Ambulance Corps during the war.

The most important part of the movement was swadeshi, which meant people would stop buying British goods, picket shops selling foreign cloth or liquor and also refuse to pay taxes. Gandhiji was passionate about the wearing of khadi, as Indian weavers were being ruined because of cheap factory-made cloth being imported from Britain. So wherever he went he asked people to take off their foreign clothes and burn them in huge bonfires. As he travelled across the country, people would throw clothes into a pile at station platforms—kurtas, coats, trousers, socks, turbans all came flying through the air, and as the train steamed out of the station the bonfires would flare up in triumph. Soon khadi clothes and Gandhi cap became the uniform of the freedom fighter and everyone was sitting with a charkha spinning cotton.

Swadeshi was a very clever idea because the British were in India to make money and now their profits were hit very badly. Also, the empire could only survive if the people cooperated with it. When taxes were not paid and no one bought British goods it hurt them economically. Moreover, the wearing of khadi became so popular that the sale of Lancashire mill cloth was reduced to half in just one year! The sale of liquor was equally badly affected with people picketing liquor shops. In fact some desperate officials in Madras came up with the bright idea of running advertisements in newspapers showing famous people like Napoleon and Shakespeare drinking, but it didn't work!

This was the time when Gandhiji made another change in his clothes. Till then he was wearing a khadi kurta, a cap or turban and a long dhoti. Then at a meeting in Madurai some students said that wearing khadi clothes was too expensive, and so he simplified it even further. Now the champion of the spinning wheel wore the unique fashion ensemble of the poorest peasant—a *chhoti si dhoti* and a khaddar chaddar. He always understood the symbolic power of an image and he now looked like a farmer; the common people loved him even more.

Gandhiji was so passionate about khadi that no one had the courage to go up to him wearing anything else. He designed the party flag with the bands of saffron, white and green and a charkha in the middle. Khadi and the spinning wheel thus became symbols of national pride, and when anyone paid four annas to become a member of the Congress they were presented with a charkha. There are photographs of party processions with a giant charkha on a cart. Wherever he was, Gandhiji spent an hour every day spinning thread and his followers would sit and spin with him—dozens of charkhas whirling away under the shade of tree.

Gandhiji was always a social reformer first, and during his travels he would usually talk to people about causes very close to his heart—religious tolerance, the fight against untouchability, the emancipation of women, education for all and the need for good nutrition and hygiene. This was the time when women gathered courage to move out of the purdah, and they marched out on the streets. They took off their jewellery and donated it to the party funds. Many leaders like Sarojini Naidu inspired them to get educated and become independent.

In many places schools, colleges, shops, law courts and banks were shut, and the country came to a halt. When thousands of people joined protest marches carrying the tricolour flag, singing patriotic songs, the government reacted with anger. The police raided party offices and peaceful marches were met by baton-wielding policemen and men on horses holding spears. People were arrested for wearing the Gandhi cap or simply saying 'Gandhiji ki jai'. For an agitation of this size there were very few episodes of violence, and simple, unarmed people showed remarkable courage. In villages farmers refused to pay taxes, workers at tea plantations in Assam walked off and the porters at Howrah station refused to carry boxes of foreign goods.

The young were the most enthusiastic satyagrahis, and many of them were expelled from schools and colleges for joining the protests. As a result national schools and colleges were opened by the Congress. Among them were the Kashi Vidyapeeth in Varanasi, the Bengal National University in Calcutta, with Subhas Chandra Bose as its first principal, and the Jamia Millia in Aligarh. Today the National University is the Jadavpur University and Jamia thrives in Delhi.

A worried viceroy, Lord Reading, invited the Prince of Wales to India hoping that it would revive the loyalty of the people. What was even more galling was that when the prince landed in Bombay, expecting to be welcomed by loyal subjects smiling and waving flags, the streets were deserted as everyone had gone off to listen to Gandhiji! So far Lord Reading had not taken the satyagraha too seriously, thinking it would soon die down. But now he was deeply embarrassed and quite furious. The government crackdown got serious and soon 30,000 people were in prison, including most of the Congress leaders, though they still did not arrest Gandhiji, worried about the public anger that would follow. This was the time when the Inner Temple in London, where Gandhiji had become a barrister, removed him from its rolls, thirty years after he had been called to the Bar and twelve years after he had stopped practising law!

Chauri Chaura

From the moment Gandhiji had started planning the campaign he had been worried about violence. So he had planned a satyagraha in stages: first the returning of awards, then boycott of school and colleges, then closing of shops and people resigning from government jobs. He was going to start a full non-cooperation agitation only if the campaign remained peaceful. He sensed a problem in Bombay when protestors beat up the people who had gone to greet the Prince of Wales. He went on a fast until peace was restored, but he was a worried man.

Then on 4 February 1922, in the village of Chauri Chaura in the Gorakhpur district of the United Provinces (modern Uttar Pradesh), people had taken out a torchlight procession and they were taunted and then fired at by a bunch of police constables. An angry mob chased the constables back to the police station, set fire to it, and twenty-two people were killed. When the news reached Gandhiji, he was devastated and immediately suspended the satyagraha. Many of his colleagues were deeply disappointed, including Jawaharlal Nehru, because they thought the campaign should not be suspended only because of one episode of violence. Gandhiji stayed firm: there was no place for violence in satyagraha, and as long as the people did not understand it, there would be no further protests.

As Gandhiji withdrew to Sabarmati Ashram, for most people this was a terrible anti-climax and there was a lot of angry criticism of his decision. The government sensing the mood immediately arrested Gandhiji and put him on trial. He defended himself in court, and when asked his profession wrote 'farmer and weaver'. As he had done at Champaran, he stood up and immediately admitted his guilt, said he was against the British empire, had asked people to break the law and then very politely requested that the judge should award him the maximum sentence for his many crimes. He said that he believed it was his moral duty to protest against an unjust government and he was willing to pay any price for it and would 'cheerfully submit to the highest penalty'.

To the astonishment of the spectators, Judge Broomfield called Gandhiji a 'great patriot and a great leader' and 'a man of high ideals and of noble and even saintly life'. He regretted that he had to follow the law as he sentenced Gandhiji to prison for six years, but hoped that the government would reduce the sentence. So instead of being jailed as a criminal, a smiling Gandhiji left the court a bigger hero! The government arrested and jailed him many times after this, but they never put him on trial, fearing it would just make him even more popular. He would be released after two years when he had to be operated for appendicitis and went back to Sabarmati to recuperate. He spent his time in prison reading, writing and spinning and probably planning the perfect non-violent satyagraha.

Did the movement fail?

When announcing the satyagraha, Gandhiji had optimistically announced that the Non-cooperation Movement would bring 'swaraj in one year'. But typically, he had been rather vague about what he meant by 'swaraj'. If it meant independence and a parliamentary government by the people, well, then that did not happen. But if it was about creating an awareness of freedom among the people, developing a freedom of the mind, then it was a great success. Indians became conscious of not just their rights but also their power. From being a hopeless, apathetic, colonized people we became a united political nation, ready to answer Gandhiji's call.

Till then most people believed that the British were so powerful they would rule India forever. Now for the first time they realized that if they stood up together, even an unarmed peaceful people could shake the most powerful empire in the world. They began to think of themselves as Indians first, not as Tamilians or Bengalis, Hindus or Muslims, upper or lower castes. Moreover, this was also the time of women's emancipation, and they could now take an energetic part in the freedom movement. We became a nation that was proud of its culture and civilization and most importantly, we stopped being afraid. As Jawaharlal Nehru said, 'Gandhiji's quiet and determined voice was raised: Be not afraid.'

While Gandhiji was in jail, some Congress leaders created the Swaraj Party and even stood for elections to the provincial legislatures, but the political scene was rather quiet. Meanwhile, a thoughtful man sat in a prison cell in Yeravda Jail, reading, writing, spinning and thinking. He came out and for the next few years became a social worker, concentrating on the spread of the message of khadi. B.R. Nanda describes one such khadi promotion trip: 'In another village he opened a khadi shop, not by delivering a speech but by sitting down with a yard measure, a pair of scissors and a cash memo book, selling the cloth and signing receipts; for an hour he sold khadi at the rate of ten rupees a minute before motoring down to the next village.'

He also worked for the equality of the Dalits and spoke up for Hindu–Muslim unity, while chiding villagers for wasting money on garlands. He was disappointed at the way people had not taken his call for ahimsa seriously and felt India was not yet ready for another satyagraha. He would plan the next all-India movement only six years later in 1930, and then it would start with—you won't believe it—a pinch of salt!

Satyagraha at Bardoli

At the time when Gandhiji stopped the Non-cooperation Movement after the incidence at Chauri Chaura, he and Vallabhbhai Patel were planning a satyagraha at a place called Bardoli. The plan was abandoned but then revived in 1928 when the villagers came to Gandhiji begging for his help. This was one of the best examples of satyagraha during the freedom movement, where people were involved, newer strategies were developed and it was all achieved without any violence. Bardoli was really the achievement of one of Gandhiji's greatest followers— the magnificent Sardar Vallabhbhai Patel.

Patel was a rich and successful lawyer in Ahmedabad who led a comfortable, Westernized life at the time when Gandhiji returned to India from South Africa. One day, Gandhiji was going to give a speech on satyagraha at the exclusive Ahmedabad Club and requested the members to attend. Patel was playing bridge with his friends when this thin, frail-looking man wearing the clothes of a peasant came up to their table. Patel listened, smiled politely and went back to his cards.

Later he read a copy of the lecture and was so intrigued that he went to listen to this strange-looking man from South Africa. Till then he had not been interested in politics, but this lawyer's mind was immediately attracted to the logical and subtle strategy to fight for freedom. He realized satyagraha was the right path for a poor, unarmed people to fight the might of an empire. He met Gandhiji and, like many others, fell under his spell and became one of his most devoted lieutenants. He gave up his successful law practice, threw away his fancy suits and put on khadi. He was Gandhiji's general in the battle for the mind and heart of Bardoli. Many years later, when both of them were in Yeravda Jail, Patel taught Gandhiji to play bridge, though we don't know if the Mahatma was any good at the game.

This satyagraha was carried out in the district of Bardoli in Gujarat where it was said the people were very gentle and even the dogs did not bark at strangers. In 1928, an Indian revenue official named Jayakar arrived in Bardoli. His job was to assess the taxes to be paid by the farmers, and to the utter shock of the people he suddenly raised the taxes by one-third. The poor peasants begged the government to think again, but as land revenue was a big source of income the officials were very reluctant to do so and only cut it to one-fourth, which was again too much. After Champaran the farmers of the country knew who to call for help and appealed to Gandhiji. He always assessed the situation himself before joining any protest, and he sent Patel to find out the real picture at Bardoli. Patel's report was that the tax was too high and the officials were being unfair. Hence they decided to revive their plan for a satyagraha in that area.

Patel moved to live in a village in Bardoli to direct a no-tax campaign. What it meant was that the farmers refused to pay all taxes till the government listened to their problems. Gandhiji and Patel had led a similar campaign in Kheda a few years before, where the taxes had been reduced, but Bardoli became a much tougher fight. The provincial government decided that it would not give in because it feared that if they agreed to the farmers' demands in Bardoli then farmers in other areas would also rise in protest. Also, the officials wanted to make an example of Bardoli by showing how tough they could be, so that no one would ever have the courage to protest again. So the battle of wills between the Bombay Government and the farmers of Bardoli began and it would go on for many difficult months.

No one thought the farmers had a chance as hundreds of villagers were arrested and jailed. The government sent in the police to confiscate land and crops and they carried away not just cattle, carts and ploughs but even the pots and pans from kitchens. Bands of armed Pathans were sent in to threaten and scare the villagers. Patel had a tough time keeping up the courage of these poor villagers and also controlling the angry young men from becoming violent and hitting back. Keeping to their vow of non-violence was the hardest part of the campaign, and once he had to stop a group of boys from laying nails on the road to deflate the tyres of the police cars!

Patel met the official actions with clever strategies. Whenever villagers saw the government agents arriving, they would run into their huts, taking their cattle with them and lock themselves in. They dismantled their carts and plough and buried them in the fields. By then the newspapers had begun to report on the battle of Bardoli and money started pouring in from all across India even as volunteers arrived to support the farmers. Then the government was embarrassed even further when factory workers in Bombay threatened to go on strike in support of the people of Bardoli.

As the satyagraha went on for months, the farmers began to suffer and some of them weakened and decided to pay the higher tax. They quickly changed their minds when they discovered that the whole village would boycott them. The families of government officials also faced a social boycott as the milkman refused to deliver milk, the vegetable seller did not stop at their houses and even the barber wouldn't cut their hair! And maids, washermen and sweepers stopped working for them. A newspaper called *Satyagraha Patrika* was published, giving daily reports of what was happening in the villages, and this kept up the hopes of the people as they felt they were part of a popular uprising.

Everyone feared that Patel would be arrested next, and so after a few months Gandhiji also moved to Bardoli, ready to take his place. Bardoli was also a true social revolution as people of different castes and religions forgot their differences and worked together. As many of the men had been arrested, the women now came out and groups of them went from house to house offering help. As a matter of fact it was these women who first began calling Vallabhbhai Patel 'Sardar', and he was always immensely proud of the title.

Finally after six long months Sardar Patel's brother Vithalbhai managed to bring the problem of Bardoli to the attention of the central government and the viceroy ordered an enquiry. The rise in taxes was cancelled, the arrested farmers were released and their land and property returned to them. The whole country heaved a joyous sigh of relief, as the simple, courageous people of Bardoli had defeated the mighty angrez sarkar! And they did it peacefully, without a single act of violence. Bardoli is the perfect example of satyagraha in action, and it proved that what Gandhiji had planned was in fact possible in reality. The violence at Chauri Chaura had filled his heart with misgivings, but the copybook satyagraha at Bardoli—disciplined, peaceful and inspiring—revived his hopes and he was ready once again to try satyagraha on a national level.

When Gandhiji had first talked about a peaceful struggle, many people had scoffed at him. They said successful freedom movements, like those in France, Russia and the United States, all involved an armed struggle. They said, you can't fight an imperial power with peaceful marches. Gandhiji's reply was that if people were determined, united and courageous, no one could defeat them. The satyagrahas of Champaran, Kheda and especially Bardoli showed that it was possible. For the first time the poor people of India realized they had a powerful weapon based on truth and courage to take on the British empire. At Bardoli Gandhiji gave power back to where it belonged—to the people.

The language of a revolution

The Indian freedom movement introduced some new words into the vocabulary of the country. These words were—satyagraha, ahimsa, swadeshi and swaraj. These words are deeply woven into the life and work of Gandhiji, and became the mantra of the Congress Party.

Gandhiji was the first to admit that none of the philosophies and strategies he talked about was originally created by him. What he did was to develop them further and at times give them a rather original Gandhian twist. Take the swadeshi campaign for example: in the beginning it meant just the burning of foreign goods, but with Gandhiji it had the country spinning at the charkha. And he connected them all into a complete programme for freedom struggle.

It was Gandhiji who thought up the word 'satyagraha' while he was in South Africa, and by the time he returned to India in 1915 he had a well-thought-out philosophy that continued to evolve throughout our freedom struggle. The word is so subtle and full of meaning for Indians that it's very hard to translate. In Sanskrit, where it originates, 'satya' is truth and 'agraha' means to hold on firmly to something. So satyagraha means to hold on to truth. But it is much more than that—it is a call to action and a way of life.

Gandhiji called it 'the Force which is born of Truth and Love or non-violence.' Others have translated it as 'soul force', 'truth force' and 'militant non-violence'. If we connect satyagraha to our freedom movement then in action it was to protest through passive resistance against unjust laws and colonial occupation. Some called it passive resistance, but Gandhiji thought that the description of a movement that was active and energetic as 'passive' was not correct and therefore created the word satyagraha.

Ahimsa or non-violence is at the heart of satyagraha and its most important weapon. When you protest, you do not pick up guns or bombs. You do not assassinate people or blow up railway tracks. Instead people walk out on the streets carrying flags, shouting slogans and singing, but they do it peacefully. When the police attack with batons, they do not hit back but they also do not give up. To be a satyagrahi required great discipline and even greater courage.

During the freedom movement this scene was repeated in the country in cities, towns and villages—a group of khadi-clad men and women faced the police armed with batons and at times guns. Anyone would think it was a very unequal struggle, but in the end it was the people who triumphed. There were many instances when police and the army men refused to fire on their own people, were dismissed and even went to prison. The government too became worried when newspapers abroad carried reports of brutalities on peaceful protestors, and there was a lot of public criticism. After a while the reputation of the great and benign British Raj was very badly affected.

Gandhiji said satyagraha was not the way of the coward—you did not run away, you did not hide; instead you conquered your fear. In most cases the protestors faced a lathi charge, were arrested, stuffed into police vans and taken to jail. Many were badly injured and faced great hardships and torture in prison, but the moment they were released they were back on the streets again. For Congressmen, getting beaten and going to prison became a proud badge of the freedom fighter. Lala Lajpat Rai died after being hit at a demonstration, and Jawaharlal Nehru spent a total of eleven years in dingy rat-infested cells and often in solitary confinement. The stories of ordinary Indians facing physical danger with such stoic courage won the admiration of the world.

Ahimsa was also a way of life for Gandhiji and he said, 'Ahimsa and love are one and the same thing.' He felt violence was an unending cycle where one act of violence led to another and an eye for an eye led to a world that was blind. His campaign against untouchability was also a form of ahimsa, and he called the supposedly 'lower castes' Harijans—the people of god. His battle against the cruelties of the caste system went on all his life. Whenever he travelled he stayed in the houses of the poorest people, who were often Dalits. He sat in dharma outside temples that did not allow them to enter as he considered untouchability a sin. When he was young he threw away his sacred thread because Dalits were not allowed to wear them. So ahimsa became the fight for equality and justice in society.

Swadeshi comes from two words—'swa', mine, and 'desh', country. So it is anything that belongs to one's own country. It became a campaign to make India self-reliant by using Indian made goods. The swadeshi movement was begun by Bal Gagadhar Tilak in 1905 during the campaign against the partition of Bengal. People burnt foreign goods, especially cloth, and began to use Indian products. The British had ruined the lives of millions of Indian weavers by bringing in cheap British mill cloth while taxing the Indian weavers. It had led to terrible poverty and misery.

Gandhiji had walked through many villages and was haunted by the hopeless poverty that he saw there. He evolved the swadeshi idea to include the spinning and weaving of khadi. He dreamed of villages with self-sufficient economies where everyone earned enough. He had also noticed that most farmers sat idle for months, and he wanted them to spin khadi and earn some money. The city-bred Congressmen, most of whom had never visited a village, thought it was another of his eccentric experiments and in the beginning no one took his proposal to support khadi very seriously.

Gandhiji realized that he would have to set a personal example and decided to start spinning on a charkha. In his autobiography *My Experiments with Truth* he admits that he hadn't seen a charkha before 1908. He then describes his struggles to get a loom working at Sabarmati Ashram and find the people to train the ashram members. The woman who taught them to spin was a tough, independent widow named Gangabai, and he was delighted to discover that she also did not believe in untouchability.

At every opportunity he asked Congressmen to use the charkha and insisted that wearing khadi was essential during the Non-cooperation Movement. When leaders like Sardar Patel and Motilal Nehru began to wear khadi and Gandhiji sat spinning during his public meetings, suddenly khadi became trendy. Weavers and mills began to produce khadi cloth, charkhas were spinning merrily in city homes and khadi became the uniform of the freedom fighter. If today we are proud of our hand woven textiles—the iridescent ikats and kanjeevarams, the delicate tangails and maheshwaris that sell across the world—it is because of the charkha and the khadi campaign.

An optimistic dreamer, Gandhiji hoped that satyagraha would one day lead to swaraj—the rule of the people—and India would become an independent country where all citizens were equal. Our constitution enshrines the basic human rights that are part of a true swaraj: the rights that we take for granted today—the right to equality, the freedom to practise one's religion, the right to vote and freedom of speech.

There had been many freedom struggles before, but India's satyagraha was unique because it was the first one to achieve freedom through peaceful means. It was the first brick to fall from the edifice of imperialism and soon colonies in Asia and Africa would become free. The nation rose in passionate protest in three great satyagrahas—the Non-cooperation Movement of 1920, the Civil Disobedience of 1930 and the Quit India Movement of 1942. The British empire had existed because the people were obedient and afraid. Satyagraha was peaceful yes, but it was rebellious and fearless and clamoured loudly and persistently for freedom.

Satyagraha puts dictators in a dilemma. A violent

protest can be met with greater violence, and they have the army and the police. But what do you do against an opponent who does not hit back? You arrest one protestor and ten more take his place, and soon your prisons are full and the country has stopped functioning! It is a campaign anyone could join—men, women and even children. In fact there was the Vanar Sena of teenagers that joined marches, and once in Nasik when the police took away their flags, the boys got shirts stitched of flags and wore them to the next demonstration!

Satyagraha united the country that was divided by religion and caste because during marches when you were out on the street shouting slogans at the top of your voice, all that mattered was that you were an Indian and it was a wonderful feeling. Indians regained their courage, confidence and self-respect and it gave us back our pride. Satyagraha made us a nation, and that is Mahatma Gandhi's greatest achievement.

6   A Long Walk to Dandi

1929–1935

He was always a man who liked to walk about among his people, and one day he went on a long march that galvanized a nation and put satyagraha back on the forefront of India's freedom struggle. Once again, the whole country was ready to follow his call for another mass struggle.

In the years after the episode at Chauri Chaura and the halting of the Non-cooperation Movement, Gandhiji withdrew from active politics and concentrated on social work. The Congress Party was busy, and one group calling itself the Swaraj Party even stood for elections to the legislatures. They hoped to oppose the government in the legislatures, but it wasn't very effective because the government never took them seriously. Also, a new conflict was brewing within the party. The older members were demanding that India be given Dominion Status, which would mean India would govern itself but remain within the British empire like Australia, South Africa and Canada. What they ignored was the fact that these were white colonies and no non-white country had ever been given Dominion Status. Meanwhile, younger members like Jawaharlal Nehru and Subhas Chandra

Bose were getting more and more impatient with begging the government for small concessions and were all ready to fight for freedom.

In 1928, after a lot of heated debates, Gandhiji suggested a compromise—if the government did not give Dominion Status within a year then the Congress would launch a civil disobedience campaign and seek freedom. At this time the government set up the Simon Commission to look into the matter, hoping to calm the growing anger among people. However, this had an opposite effect and brought the freedom movement to life again. The main reason was that the Simon Commission had no Indian member, though it was going to decide the future of the country. Simon was welcomed with hartals and people carrying banners saying, 'Simon Go Back!' At one such peaceful demonstration at Lahore, Lala Lajpat Rai was hit by the police and later died of injuries, which only aggravated the anger among people. A shrewd judge of public mood, Gandhiji knew the country was ready for another satyagraha.

By the banks of the Ravi

The realization was growing that politely asking the British to please leave India was never going to work, and one year later Dominion Status was still nowhere in sight. In December 1929, when the Congress held its annual session in Lahore, the party symbolically passed on the flame to the next generation when Jawaharlal Nehru was elected the president. On the first day, with his typical love for drama, he led the procession on a white horse like a warrior going off to battle. At midnight on a freezing New Year Eve, by the banks of the river Ravi, he unfurled the tricolour flag and a momentous resolution was passed that said that from now on the goal of the party was 'Poorna Swaraj' or complete independence. Also, from then on, 26 January was to be celebrated as Poorna Swaraj Day.

The Congress decided to launch a campaign of civil disobedience to be led by Gandhiji, who was going to set the programme and plan the strategy of the protests. On 26 January people flew the tricolour all across India and vowed to fight for freedom and waited for Gandhiji to tell them how the satyagraha was to be carried out. That day we began a tradition that we still celebrate today. Twenty years later the new constitution of free India came into force on 26 January 1950, and from then on we celebrate it as our Republic Day.

Planning a satyagraha

Now the next challenge was how this satyagraha was to be carried out. As always that difficult task of planning was left to Gandhiji. All through the early months of 1930, as everyone watched anxiously, the master strategist wandered moodily around Sabarmati Ashram, brooding and planning. He wrote to his friend, the poet Rabindranath Tagore, 'I am furiously thinking day and night. And I do not see any light coming out of the surrounding darkness.'

This campaign would be similar in many ways to the Non-cooperation Movement. Schools, colleges, offices, courts and shops would be shut. Foreign goods were to be burnt, farmers would refuse to pay taxes, government employees and people in the army and police would quit from their jobs. At the same time Congressmen would lead peaceful marches and hold meetings, and it was their job to ensure that it all remained peaceful.

This time Gandhiji wanted to add a new element to the satyagraha. He wanted the people to deliberately break a law and provoke the government into arresting them, but at the same time the law had to be broken without any violence. So he needed a law that could be broken easily and also one that everyone understood and resented. So he began to look for an unpopular tax that everyone could refuse to pay and do it peacefully.

The final answer startled and puzzled everyone—salt!

In fact, his choice of the Salt Tax was an inspired one. It was a very small amount and a tiny part of the government revenue, but it had to be paid by everyone. So even a penniless labourer had to pay for something he needed to survive. It was like taxing food, water or air. No one except the government was allowed to make or sell salt. It was so strictly enforced that people living close to the sea were fined if they picked up a lump of sea salt lying on the beach. Gandhiji explained his plan by saying, 'The state can reach even the starving millions, the sick, the maimed and the utterly helpless. The tax constitutes therefore the most inhuman poll tax the ingenuity of man can devise.'

So how was the law to be broken? At a morning meeting at Sabarmati Ashram he unveiled his plan and said that they would all go on a march. He and a chosen band of ashram members would walk from the ashram in Ahmedabad, across Gujarat, to the seashore at Dandi where they would pick up lumps of salt from the sand and sell them. This would start the satyagraha and people across the country would start making and selling salt. Then the other satyagraha activities of boycotts, hartals and protests would follow.

The plan was a masterly act of publicity that made people sit up and watch a bunch of walkers for nearly a whole month. Till then the press abroad had not taken the Indian freedom movement too seriously, and the British press had rarely covered India's freedom struggle. But the news of a man walking for twenty-five days to make salt fascinated the press. This story was too good to miss, and reporters were soon flying in from across the world. At this time the correspondent of a British-owned paper was sent to Ahmedabad to report on the 'enemy camp', and to his discomfort he was politely invited into Sabarmati and taken around as an honoured guest.

It took a while for the idea to sink in as even his most devoted followers muttered to each other, 'Salt? Why make salt?' Government officials thought it was ridiculous because the tax was in fact quite a small amount and would not hurt their earnings. As the historian B.R. Nanda writes, they 'laughed away the idea that the King-Emperor could be unseated by boiling sea-water in a kettle.' Even Jawaharlal was puzzled and wrote later, 'Salt suddenly became a mysterious word, a word of power . . . we were bewildered and could not fit in a national struggle with common salt.'

What they missed was the simplicity of the idea. As Gandhiji explained it, 'Supposing ten men in each of the 7,00,000 villages in India came forward to manufacture salt and to disobey the Salt Act, what do you think this government can do?' Everyone, even the illiterate poor, could understand it and this would make everyone join the satyagraha. It would create a national uprising and force the government to take them seriously. One man understood him immediately, his old friend C. Rajagopalachari, a shrewd lawyer and comrade in many battles, who told him, 'It's not salt but disobedience that you are manufacturing.'

Gandhiji planned the satyagraha like a military campaign. Everything was done by letters, telegrams and by telephone, and leaders travelled across the country to meet local Congress people. At the same time funds had to be raised and the marchers had to be selected and trained. Every village on the route was sent instructions on the kind of shelters to be built and what food was to be cooked. He knew exactly how many miles they had to walk each day and the time when they would arrive at a village.

He wrote, 'If provisions are supplied, the party will cook its own meal. The food supplied should be the simplest possible . . . sweets even if prepared will be declined. Vegetables should be merely boiled and no oil or spice to be added.' Then he suggested the menu—simple Gujarati dishes like rotli, khichadi, rab, dhebra, bhakri and buttermilk. Exactly three tolas of ghee would be used per head and his own diet was of goat's milk, raisins, dates and three lemons each day.

Once he was ready to move, he sent a polite letter to the viceroy Lord Irwin announcing his plans and addressing him as 'My Dear Friend'. Irwin did not respond to his demands, but as the letter was printed in every newspaper, the whole country now knew of Gandhiji's plans. The Dandi March, followed by the Salt Satyagraha, was first a brilliant piece of showmanship and then a very well-organized national campaign. It succeeded where non-cooperation had failed by remaining remarkably peaceful, and it was more effective because it involved more people. It was mass satyagraha at its best.

The Dandi March

On 12 March 1930, everyone at Sabarmati Ashram was awake well before dawn. As a matter of fact no one had really slept the night before except Gandhiji. As everyone sang bhajans, Gandhiji and seventy-eight ashram members streamed out of the ashram. There were some tearful eyes and many of them had said their goodbyes because they thought they wouldn't come back alive. Kasturba wanted to go along and began to walk with them, but was persuaded by Gandhiji to stay back. Of

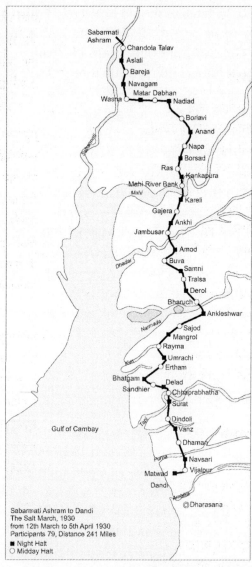

The following labels appear on the map:

Sabarmati
Ashram
Chandola Talav
Aslali
Bareja
Navagam
Matar Dabhan
Washa
Nadiad
Boriavi
Anand
Napa
Borsad
Ras
Kankapura
Mahi River Bank
Mahi
Kareli
Gajera
Ankhi
Jambusar
Amod
Buva
Samni
Tralsa
Derol
Bharuch
Ankleshwar
Narmada
Sajod
Mangrol
Rayma
Umrachi
Ertham
Bhatgam
Delad
Sandhier
Chhaprabhatha
Surat
Dindoli
Vanz
Dhaman
Navsari
Matwad
Vijalpur
Dandi
Dharasana
Gulf of Cambay

Sabarmati Ashram to Dandi
The Salt March, 1930
from 12th March to 5th April 1930
Participants 79, Distance 241 Miles
■ Night Halt
○ Midday Halt

The Route of Gandhiji's March from
Sabarmati Ashram to Dandi

course they could have taken a train or bus to Dandi, but instead they decided to walk for twenty-five days, letting the excitement grow and grow.

We have a detailed list of the marchers, all young men, fit for a long and arduous walk. The youngest, Vitthal Thakkar, was sixteen; the oldest, a Mr M.K. Gandhi from Gujarat, was sixty. They had been carefully selected and belonged to every caste, community and region. They also included two from Nepal, two Indians who came back from the United States, one who was born in Fiji and another who gave up a successful business in London. There were students, teachers, weavers, mill workers, leather workers, businessmen, scientists, medical students, a postman, a bhajan singer and Gandhiji's son Manilal and grandson Kantilal.

It was early summer and the heat was rising, so every day they began their march at dawn, ate lunch and rested at a village during the afternoon, resuming their walk in the evening, to spend the night at the next village. Gandhiji was one of the fastest walkers, and even though someone had supplied a horse for him he never rode it. At the villages where they stopped for lunch or dinner Gandhiji spoke to the people, kept a diary, answered his mail and even found time to spin. It was 400 km to Dandi and it took them twenty-five days to cover the distance. What was most amusing was that the leading marcher had not taken any salt in his food for years!

Carrying his tall stick, he strode on along dusty village paths, past fields of wheat and mustard and ponds shining silver in the sun, and crossing rivers by boat. People sprinkled water and laid leaves on the stony village tracks and welcomed them with banners and arches. Rows of them sat at whirling charkhas and sang Gandhiji's favourite bhajans to the beat of the marcher's feet. Even though he had forbidden people to follow, no one listened and the crowd kept growing until it looked like a white river snaking across the countryside. By the time they reached Dandi they were in thousands with many reporters and photographers among them.

No one captures the scene better than Jawaharlal Nehru, who wrote lyrically, 'Many pictures rise in my mind of this man, whose eyes were often full of laughter and yet were pools of infinite sadness. But the picture that is dominant and most significant is as I saw him marching, staff in hand, to Dandi on the Salt March in 1930; here was the pilgrim on his quest of truth, quiet, peaceful, determined and fearless, who could continue that quest and pilgrimage regardless of consequences.'

The viceroy, Lord Irwin, had optimistically hoped that a sixty-year-old man would surely fall ill and stop walking. When he heard that, Gandhiji laughed and said, 'Less than twelve miles a day in two stages with not much luggage—child's play!' Everyone waited to see how the government would respond, but in fact it could do little except wait as no law had been broken yet. They had earlier arrested Patel for giving a speech and on his way to jail he had stopped to say goodbye to Gandhiji at Sabarmati and joked that he was going to keep a prison cell ready for his old friend.

On 5 April 1930 they arrived at the seashore at Dandi and Gandhiji picked up a handful of sea salt mixed with sand and launched the satyagraha. Later this mix of salt and sand was sold at an auction. Immediately all across India people marched to the seashore or boiled salt water in pans to make salt and sold it. Actually most of this salt was unusable, but they did break the law. Finally the government moved and arrested Gandhiji and he was taken to Yeravda Jail. Satyagraha started everywhere and within a few months 60,000 people were in prison.

Peaceful marches were met by the police carrying batons and rifles and men riding on horses carrying spears. People were arrested on false charges of theft or rioting and given long sentences; many of them even faced beatings in prison. Sometimes even the armed forces protested at the violence unleashed by the government, like the soldiers of the Royal Garhwal Regiment at Peshawar who refused to fire on unarmed people and many were sentenced to life imprisonment. As the satyagraha spread to the countryside, the government became nervous and began beating and arresting villagers and taking away land and crops. Many Indian newspapers were banned, but people brought out handwritten sheets to spread the news.

Kasturba led women into picketing shops selling foreign goods and liquor and they led prabhat pheris— singing through the streets at dawn. Many of them were arrested and jailed. The womenfolk would also nurse those hurt during the demonstrations. This was the time when Motilal Nehru donated his mansion in Allahabad,

Anand Bhawan, to the cause. It was renamed Swaraj Bhawan and turned into a hospital. Teenage boys formed the Vanar Sena or monkey brigade, so girls started the Manjari Sena or cat army.

At Dharsana

The finest act of peaceful satyagraha took place at the Dharsana Salt Works in Gujarat. The picket was led by Sarojini Naidu as Gandhiji had been arrested. On 21 May 1930, she led 2,000 satyagrahis to the factory which had been surrounded by barbed wire and was guarded by policemen. What followed shocked the world. Under the scorching sun, in complete silence, groups of men walked up to the barricades and tried to enter. As they were beaten by the police, many fell to the ground bleeding from wounds, and volunteers ran up to carry them away to a first-aid station. The only sound to be heard was the sickening thud of sticks landing on bodies and cries of pain and the running feet of volunteers. Over 300 satyagrahis were injured and two were killed, but not one man raised even a fist in retaliation.

The police, expecting trouble, had stopped all passenger trains to Dharsana, but one intrepid American reporter Webb Miller hitched a ride on a goods train and walked seven miles to get there. His report was carried across the world as he wrote about the horrific scene, 'Not one of the marchers even raised an arm to fend off the blows . . . in eighteen years of my reporting, in twenty countries, during which I have witnessed innumerable civil disturbances, riots, street fights and rebellions; I have never witnessed such harrowing scenes as at Dharsana.'

The country could never forgive such brutality and the world finally saw the real face of imperialism. These men proved that satyagraha needed immense courage and discipline and it is not the path of the meek or the coward. And that a true satyagraha wins the hearts and minds of the people.

In London

The government was aware of the hold the Congress had acquired over people and began to fear that civil disobedience would spread to the police and army. Finally in early 1931 Irwin invited Gandhiji for a series of talks. As the Mahatma travelled from Yeravda Jail and then walked into the new Viceregal Palace on Raisina Hill in New Delhi, the significance of the moment was not lost on anyone. Representatives of the mighty Raj and the Congress were meeting as equals, not as imperial power and a subject nation. What followed was the Gandhi–Irwin Pact, according to which peaceful picketing was allowed, prisoners were to be released, salt could be manufactured for personal use and Gandhiji was to attend the second Round Table Conference in London.

Gandhiji travelled by ship, by the lowest class, and spent most of his time on deck reading, spinning and playing with children. They disembarked at Marseilles in France and then travelled by train to London. At the

Gare de Lyon station in Paris an admirer tried to bring a goat for his milk diet, but the police stopped him!

The conference did not achieve anything because the British were not even willing to consider Dominion Status. Also, there was no unity among the Indians who were only keen to safeguard the interest of their own communities. There were leaders representing not just Muslims, Sikhs and Christians, but also maharajas, Dalits and even planters and Anglo-Indians. They left the hard job of fighting for freedom to the Congress and were already squabbling for the spoils. In fact the only man in the room who truly represented a majority of Indians was Gandhiji, and he received no support from the other Indian leaders.

Gandhiji was a hit in London as reporters followed him everywhere. He addressed many meetings and even met the mill workers of Lancashire, who were facing problems because of the khadi campaign. Many mills had closed and they had lost their jobs when sales of mill cloth fell in India. In his speech he explained the reason for the khadi campaign by saying, 'You have 3 million unemployed but we have 300 million unemployed for half the year. Your average unemployment dole is 70 shillings. Our average income is 7 shillings and 6 pence a month.' The workers greeted his speech with applause and he was photographed with smiling workers.

Gandhiji stayed in London's East End, a poor locality, and soon was very popular with the children there. When he was leaving they presented him with 'two woolly dogs, three pink birthday candles, a tin plate, a blue pencil and some jelly sweets' which he happily carried back to India. He met many people, including the playwright George Bernard Shaw, and film star Charlie Chaplin came to meet him. The Mahatma, who never watched films, did not even know who he was! He went for tea with George V and as always wore his usual chaddar-dhoti-chappal fashion ensemble and this shocked many conservative people. When asked by a reporter if he felt inappropriately dressed for the occasion, he gave his toothy grin and said, 'The king had enough on for both of us.' His finest riposte was to the question, 'Mr Gandhi, what do you think of Western civilization?' He nodded his bald head and replied solemnly, 'That would be a good idea.'

The satyagraha was resumed when he came back, but it was losing steam and he withdrew it in 1934. Also, Irwin had been replaced by Lord Willingdon as viceroy and he was not interested in continuing with the Gandhi–Irwin Pact. Gandhiji was arrested again and went back to spinning in Yeravda Jail. With his usual serenity he discovered newer ways to occupy himself, began to study astronomy and spent his nights watching the stars.

The government reluctantly realized that Indians had to be given some power and hence brought a new act in 1935 by which people could elect their own governments in the provinces. However, it was not a real democracy as very few people were allowed to vote; women did not vote at all. In fact only one-sixth of the people had the rights to vote. Moreover, the viceroy and the provincial governors still controlled the important departments. Though very unhappy with the act, the Congress decided to contest the elections to be held in 1937.

A Dandi diary

- Including Gandhiji, seventy-nine marchers walked from 12 March to 5 April 1930, from Sabarmati Ashram in Ahmedabad to Dandi on the Arabian Sea. They walked around 24 km every day and covered 400 km in twenty-five days.
- Because of the Salt Tax, the price of salt was eighty times its actual cost of production.
- Gandhiji's walking stick was a gift from Kaka Kalelkar, the principal of the Gujarat Vidyapeeth School. It was a fifty-four inches long, iron-tipped, lacquered bamboo staff.
- At one place a brass band waiting to welcome them got a bit confused and began to play 'God Save the King' by mistake!
- At a few villages where the headman did not approve of the march, they got a lukewarm welcome and had to organize their own food and shelter.
- The Arun Tukdi was a group of students who went ahead and prepared a village to receive the marchers.
- The marchers were followed by two bullock carts carrying khadi cloth to be sold, charkhas to be distributed and Gandhiji's commode!
- Pandit Khare carried his tanpura and sang at every stop.

- There were police spies in the crowd, and at one village a policeman found that his car would not start as someone had messed with its carburettor.
- At one village Gandhiji refused to speak until Harijans were allowed into the pandal.
- At the end of the month, most of the marchers were in good health; Gandhiji gained two pounds in weight, though his rheumatism bothered him.
- Gandhiji only used salt in his tooth powder and as a nasal douche.
- While crossing the river Mahi, so many people jumped into his boat that it nearly sank. Then they had to wade through knee-deep mud at the other side.
- When fishermen at Kankapura were threatened by the police, a farmer bought a boat and ferried the marchers across the river.
- A dentist at Broach treated the young marchers to ice cream and Gandhiji was not pleased.
- In 1970, seventy-nine students of the Gujarat Vidyapeeth repeated the march as a part of the celebrations of Gandhiji's birth centenary.
- A Gandhian scholar from Australia, Thomas Weber, did the march in 1983 and wrote a book about it.

7 🚶 'Do or Die!'
1937–1942

The huge popular response to the Salt Satyagraha all across the country sent a very clear message to the British government—if they refused to listen to the voice of the Indian people, then the Congress had the power and the ability to start another mass movement. So if the government did not want the country to come to a halt again, they had to give Indians more power.

Even though the British were constantly harping on how they ruled India for the welfare of the Indians, people now realized that it was nothing of the sort. They were here to make money. Indian taxes paid for the affluent lives of the British people and their royalty, and also the fat pensions of retired bureaucrats and soldiers. In fact, officers in India were better paid than their counterparts in Britain and the Indian viceroy earned more than the British prime minister! The Indian market kept the British factories churning out goods and Indians were forced to buy them as industries were not encouraged in the country. The Salt Satyagraha and the khadi campaign proved very effectively how a satyagraha could be economically harmful for Britain. So very reluctantly, in 1935, an act of parliament was passed that allowed Indians to fight elections and form governments, though only in the provinces.

The Act of 1935 was opposed by many in the British parliament, including Winston Churchill, at that time a member of parliament, who was violently against giving Indians any form of self-government. In fact, the Indian ministers in the provincial governments had little power as only unimportant ministries were given to them. The important departments like finance and security were controlled by the governors, who could dismiss ministers at will. The viceroy remained the supreme lord and master of the empire, controlling most of the budget and with the power to veto anything the Indian ministers proposed. As B.R. Nanda comments ironically, the Act of 1935 'was as if a motor vehicle had been set in motion in low gear with brakes on.'

In 1936 the Congress met in Lucknow and the main topic of debate was, should they fight the elections or not. Younger leaders like Jawaharlal Nehru and Subhas Chandra Bose wanted to boycott it, but the voices of older and more mature leaders finally prevailed. It was decided that the Congress would contest the elections to prove to the government that they were the only party that represented a majority of Indians. Gandhiji also felt it was an opportunity to start some social reforms and do positive things in neglected areas like primary education and health care. Moreover, the leaders wanted to show the British that they were capable of running an administration as well as the angrez sarkar.

Rise of communal parties

This was the time when many communal parties came to the forefront of Indian politics. A communal political party is never a national party because it only works for the interest of one community and these can be based on religion, region or even caste. Such communal organizations had begun to rise in the 1920s and now at the elections of 1937 they came to the fore. Most of them were based on religion, like the Muslim League, the Hindu Mahasabha or the Rashtriya Swayam Sevak Sangh (RSS). These parties did their utmost to create distrust and hatred between religions so that they could win votes. As they tried to divide people, especially the Hindus and Muslims, the British were delighted. Here was the perfect weapon to fight the growing influence of the Congress.

The Muslim League was started by a group of rich landowners who were against the Congress as it wanted land reforms and supported the rights of peasants. They declared their loyalty to the Crown and never talked of freedom or equality. Then Muhammad Ali Jinnah quit the Congress and became the president of the Muslim League and very cleverly added religion to the brew. His strategy was to create fear among the Muslims about an independent India ruled by a Hindu majority. He started calling the Congress a 'Hindu' party and declared that if the Congress came to power the Muslims would suffer. Soon he declared that not just Muslims but Islam itself was in danger from the Congress and that Muslims needed a separate state of their own that they began to call Pakistan.

Jinnah never proved in any election that the Muslim League had the support of the majority of Muslims of the country, and he knew that most Muslims did not support him. His tactic was the threat of violence, and soon he was talking of a civil war between the Hindus and the Muslims if Pakistan was not created. Throughout the 1940s horrific communal riots took place across the country and Gandhiji struggled to establish peace. All his life he had dreamed of a free India that was a rainbow nation where people of all religions lived in harmony. This was the time when that dream began to shatter.

The Hindu communal organizations made the situation worse, with people like M.S. Golwalkar of the RSS shouting that independent India would be a Hindu nation where Muslims would have to live as second-class citizens. As a result more Muslims began to support the League. The Hindu communal parties also declared, rather confusingly, that Jinnah's 'Hindu' Congress Party in fact supported the Muslims! Of course none of the communal parties were actually interested in the hard task of fighting for freedom, facing the police batons and going to jail. So it became even more important for the Congress to win the 1937 elections and prove that they represented every Indian of every religion, gender and caste.

The first election

It was not really a general election like we know it, where every Indian over the age of eighteen can vote. There were various conditions and only about one-sixth of the population voted. Led by an energetic Jawaharlal Nehru, the Congress began a nationwide campaign. In fact the roots of our democracy go back to this campaign as the leaders travelled across the country teaching people about their rights as citizens. The Congress swept the polls, forming ministries in most of the provinces while the Muslim League did very badly, not able to win even in the provinces where the Muslims were in a majority. Gandhiji urged ministers to cultivate 'industry, ability, integrity, impartiality and an infinite capacity for mastering details'. He had never wanted power for himself and went back to his social work in villages.

The Congress ministers performed remarkably well, showing high standards of honesty and efficiency. They lowered their salaries and travelled by second and third class on trains. The Temple Entry Bill, one of Gandhiji's personal interests, was passed opening temples to people of all castes and religions. Jinnah tried to form coalition governments with the Congress, but was asked to merge with the Congress instead, which he refused.

The Second World War

In 1939, the Second World War broke out in Europe where England and France were fighting Nazi Germany, and the political situation in India changed. Suddenly one morning India woke up to discover that it was also at war. The viceroy had joined the war on behalf of all Indians without even bothering to consult the Indian leaders when white dominion states like Australia, Canada and South Africa were allowed to decide for themselves. And the irony that was not lost on Indians was that Britain claimed to be fighting for freedom and democracy!

The Congress ministers resigned in protest but the Muslim League did not, loudly proclaiming their loyalty to the Crown. The day the Congress resigned, the League celebrated it as 'Day of Deliverance'. This time Gandhiji did not offer his support for the war and the party started a campaign of 'individual satyagraha' where leaders gave speeches criticizing the government and got themselves arrested. Many historians feel that these resignations were a mistake because it made the government even more suspicious of the Congress. Meanwhile the League, playing the loyalty card, developed very close relations with the British. This came very useful for Jinnah during the talks before independence and the partition of the country.

In Europe the war was not going well for Britain and its allies. By 1941 Japan had joined Germany, and its armies swept across Asia conquering one British colony after another. Singapore fell and then Burma, and soon the war was at India's borders. What worried the British was that when the Japanese entered Burma they were welcomed by the Burmese as liberators and the same could happen in India. Prime Minister Winston Churchill, who was adamantly against giving any powers to Indians, finally had to admit that he could no longer ignore the freedom struggle. The United States had joined the war on the side of the Allies and they supported the right of self-government for all nations. Both US President Roosevelt and Chiang Kai-shek of China urged Britain to talk to Indian leaders about the future of the country.

The war years were a battle of wills between Gandhiji and Churchill, and Gandhiji's biographer Louis Fischer, comparing the characters of the two men, wrote, 'Churchill loved social traditions, Gandhi smashed social barriers. Churchill mixed with every class, but lived in his own. Gandhi lived with everybody. To Gandhi, the lowliest Indian was a child of God. To Churchill, all Indians were the pedestal for a throne. He would have died to keep England free, but was against those who wanted India free.'

A new mission under Sir Stafford Cripps arrived in India in 1942 aiming to win the support of Indians by offering Dominion Status after the war. However, Cripps had a very difficult time because of the opposition from both Churchill and the viceroy Lord Linlithgow. So all that the Congress heard were vague promises of the 'earliest possible realization of self-government' and it was as always too little, too late. Gandhiji described the Cripps' offer as a 'post dated cheque' and the Congress rejected it.

By 1942 India was in turmoil. The war meant shortages of everything, from food to clothes and even paper and pencils. Prices rose higher and higher and there was a terrible famine in Bengal because of bad management. Fears rose of an invasion when the Japanese bombed Visakhapatnam; then the Japanese army was at the borders of Assam and people began to flee from

Bengal in panic. The Congress took note of the rising public anger and decided it was time to act again.

Bharat chhoro!

After the Dandi March Gandhiji had said that he would not return to Sabarmati Ashram until India became free. He then started another ashram near Wardha in Maharashtra. Here the Congress committee met in July 1942 to plan another satyagraha just before the annual session of the party that was to be held in Bombay. On 8 August 1942, on a rainy monsoon morning, Gandhiji addressed a huge gathering at Gowala Tank. Speaking of future plans he said that this was the time to start the final struggle for freedom. He said, India was no longer willing to wait, and demanded independence immediately, 'this very night before dawn if it can be had.'

His speech electrified the listening people as he went on, 'You may take it from me that I am not going to strike a bargain with the viceroy for ministries and the like. I am not going to be satisfied with anything short of complete freedom. Here is a mantra, a short one that I give you. You may imprint it on your hearts and let every breath of yours give expression to it. The mantra is "do or die". We shall either free India or die in the attempt. We shall not live to see the perpetuation of our slavery . . .'

Many historians feel Gandhiji had not really planned to start a nationwide satyagraha immediately and was only threatening to start one to make the government come to the negotiating table and talk to the Congress.

It is true that unlike the non-cooperation and the Salt Satyagraha he had not made any plans or prepared the party workers. He knew the government was under pressure because of the war, and expected them to agree to the Congress demands.

The viceroy Lord Linlithgow, armed with special wartime powers, was in no mood to talk. The police moved swiftly and at the crack of dawn the next day, all the members of the Congress Working Committee were arrested, bundled into trains and whisked off to unknown destinations. The Congress Party was banned and the whole movement was suddenly left leaderless. Gandhiji, his secretary Mahadev Desai, Sarojini Naidu and Mira Behn were taken to the Aga Khan Palace in Poona. Others like Jawaharlal Nehru, Sardar Patel and Maulana Abul Kalam Azad were imprisoned behind the grim walls of the nearby Ahmednagar Fort. They would all stay imprisoned till the war ended in 1945.

Both Gandhiji and Linlithgow had underestimated each other. Gandhiji had thought that when the Congress threatened a satyagraha, the government busy with the war would give in and start talks. Linlithgow's response to the Congress challenge was to promptly remove the leadership from the scene. He thought that a headless movement would die down soon after. During the Quit India Movement or the Bharat Chhoro Andolan, the spontaneous reaction of the people surprised them all.

The public anger at the arrest of the leaders was instant. It was the first completely people's movement that was often led by local leaders. It was unplanned, without much discipline and often descended into violence, but it enveloped a large part of the country. Angry demonstrators came out into the streets and targeted government property—railway stations, post offices, police stations and law courts that were set on fire. As Gandhiji watched helplessly, the satyagraha descended into anarchy. In the first week itself 250 railway stations, 500 post offices and 150 police stations were destroyed, and fifty-nine trains were derailed. This mindless violence made him very angry and he commented acidly that people were mistaken if they thought evil resided in bridges and roads and not in men. But he was in prison and could do nothing to control the situation.

This sudden upsurge of rage caught the authorities by surprise, and there were areas like Ballia (Uttar Pradesh) and Darbhanga (Bihar) where people took over the administration and ran parallel governments called jatiya sarkars. Many young leaders like Ram Manohar Lohia, Aruna Asaf Ali, Sucheta Kripalani and Biju Patnaik went underground, and a young Jayprakash Narayan escaped from prison to lead the movement. These were very exciting times and the whole country was galvanized into action, spontaneously marching out into the streets, defying the police and printing posters and leaflets to spread the message of rebellion.

For a while things went out of their hands, but soon the government hit back. The army was called in and protestors not only faced batons and rifles but machine guns firing from aircraft as if it was a war. There were pitched battles on the streets and though there are no official records, thousand were injured or killed and the prisons filled up again. Linlithgow admitted later that it was 'the most serious rebellion since 1857'. However, a leaderless, unplanned public uprising that has no central coordination can only face an army for a short time. The Quit India Movement was crushed within a few months and the country was quiet by the end of 1942.

Meanwhile, with all the Congress leaders in prison, the Muslim League took over the ministries in the provinces and won the support of the government. It also worked hard to win over the Muslims so that at the following elections they won a majority of seats reserved for Muslims. Jinnah anticipated that some form of freedom would be offered to India after the war was over and began to talk of a separate Muslim homeland of Pakistan. From 1942 onwards Gandhiji had a new battle to fight, to somehow keep India from breaking apart, and this time his opponent was not the British but a fellow Indian. The implacable Jinnah was a man with an iron will, who felt no regret at destroying a nation, and he was willing to use every threat to gain his purpose.

The Quit India Movement was widespread and created much excitement, but it was also violent and uncontrolled. It was very different from the ideal of a satyagraha. Even within the Congress there was disagreement about whether it had been a good idea to announce an agitation in the middle of a war. It led to all of them being removed from the scene for years and allowed the League to build up its popularity among

Muslims. Many Congress members felt Gandhiji had made a mistake and there was criticism at party meetings. It was at this time that Gandhiji gradually withdrew from the activities of the party and many historians think that this was the time when his political influence began to wane.

The Aga Khan Palace

The internment at the Aga Khan Palace from 1942–44 was the last time Gandhiji was imprisoned and it was also a time of great personal tragedy. First his loyal, old friend and long-time secretary Mahadev Desai died. Kasturba had threatened to lead the protest and forced the government to arrest her and she had joined Gandhiji at the palace. In the winter of 1943 her bronchitis became very serious and she died on 22 February 1944. When he was released in 1944, Gandhiji found a country quiet but simmering with anger after months of violence. He was a very disappointed and tired man and quietly withdrew from active politics and went back to Sewagram. From then on, all the negotiations with the government were handled by other leaders.

Bapu in the villages

It was while walking from village to village in the Champaran district of Bihar that Gandhiji came face to face with rural poverty for the first time. The hopeless lives of the villagers shocked him to the core. Kasturba, who was with him, met a family where the women possessed only one sari each and lived in that one dirty garment till it was in tatters. They saw the empty huts without a stick of furniture, kitchens with few pots, the filthy streets with open sewers and the constant fear of hunger stalking the land. Gandhiji never got over the experience, and the welfare of Indian villagers and finding a solution to their poverty became a constant challenge for him.

He was the first national leader to go deep into the countryside where he sat and listened to peasants, and what he heard turned him into a crusader. For the rest of his life he worked ceaselessly to improve their lives. He knew that this was the real India where 85 per cent of Indians lived and it was pointless talking about freedom, democracy and human rights when people were not sure of getting even one meal a day. How could they become a part of the freedom struggle when they were illiterate, burdened with work and afraid, and did not even understand what democracy meant?

During his wanderings Gandhiji noticed that farmers sat idle for many months every year once the sowing of crops was over. This was when he wove in the idea of khadi into the old swadeshi campaign. He spread the message that Indians were not only to use Indian products but those made in villages. He started the All India Spinners Association and began to distribute charkhas, encouraging village men and women to spin thread and weave cloth. He also hoped that it would revive India's dying textile industry which had always been based in the villages.

Today when the world is dazzled by the intricate craftsmanship and variety of Indian textiles, we must remember that it all began with Bapu distributing charkhas to villagers and making leaders start spinning daily to spread the message, else these traditional weaving arts would have died out much earlier They were being systematically killed by high taxes and cheaper British factory products. The weavers of Dacca, who were famous for their fine muslin, were dying in slums because they had no work. The khadi campaign slowly breathed life into these beautiful crafts.

It is hard to imagine Bapu as a fashion icon, but he sent a message when he was photographed walking into Buckingham Palace in his dhoti and chaddar. He was always a shrewd judge of the message a picture could convey, and knew that when a man from a colonized nation wore his traditional garments to meet a king he was being fearless and also proud of his own heritage. What he was saying with his impish grin was that his khaddar chaddar was just as good as the king's medal-encrusted uniform! The khadi campaign made the wearing of handlooms both patriotic and trendy. At political rallies people saw the handsome Maulana Azad and Jawaharlal Nehru in natty achkans and Subhas Bose in an elegant flowing dhoti, and they too began to wear khadi. When Sarojini Naidu swished up on stage in kanjeevaram saris in brilliant peacock hues, suddenly the socialites of Bombay began to discard their French chiffons for handlooms.

Gandhiji wanted villages to be self-reliant—growing their own food, weaving their own clothes and making their own pots and pans. He spoke constantly about living simply and believed that we should only use the earth's bounty as much as we need. He opposed the senseless cutting of trees and the destruction of forests. He said, 'The earth has enough for our needs but not enough for our greed,' and remember he said this at a time when no one was talking of the threats to the environment or the dangers of climate change. And he showed this through his own simple life. All his earthly possessions could be packed into a single cloth jhola bag. He travelled light. There were his dhotis, chaddar, his rosary beads, a tin bowl, plate and spoon. And also his spare glasses, false teeth and a copy of the Bhagwad Gita.

From the time he returned to India in 1914, his life became one of ceaseless work as he travelled across the land, often walking. At every village where he stayed he would talk of how the villagers could improve their lives. He tried to break their apathy by teaching them about hygiene and cleanliness, guided them towards cooking nutritious meals, the need to build schools to educate their children, the equality of women and against untouchability. He was keenest on hygiene and the need for clean toilets because he knew that if the sweepers did not have to clean them, then slowly the stigma of untouchability would fade away. Sadly even today many village homes lack toilets.

Even during the Dandi March, at every village where they stopped, he spoke of ways in which villages could become self-reliant—dig canals, build roads and schools, clean their streets, start small-scale industries like weaving, making baskets, pottery, metal and leather work. What is really amusing is that the government, which did not trust Gandhiji at all, even looked at his social work with great suspicion. Officials and the police were convinced that under the guise of social work he was in fact building up an army of rural satyagrahis!

If you think villagers always listened and obeyed Bapu you would be mistaken. Many of them in fact looked at him with suspicion and were angered by his talk of the rights of the lower castes and of women. Also, many of them did not know how to help themselves and Gandhiji realized that he needed volunteers from the cities to go to work in the villages. Among these volunteers were people like Vinoba Bhave and Baba Thakkar. So all the Non-government Organisations (NGOs) working in villages today are really carrying on the work he began. Today's Khadi Gramodyogs, Cottage Industries emporia, Dilli Haats and crafts melas are really a continuation of his campaigns, and they provide livelihood to millions of crafts people.

He called the village improvement campaigns 'a plodder's work'—slow, laborious and needing endless patience, but he persisted with it for thirty years. The poor were never far from his thoughts. It is easy for a politician to strut into a village, stand before a microphone, give a lot of advice at the top of his voice and drive off in a big car. Do you think they are taken seriously? The villagers listen politely to his 'bhashan', shake their heads in amusement and go back to their hard lives. They do not trust politicians.

Bapu walked the talk. Not only did he live simply, he also moved to live in a village. He chose a tiny village called Segaon near Wardha in Maharashtra and in 1936 built a hut there. Segaon had no shops, no post office or school and no roads, forget about electricity or telephones. Slowly a whole community of people interested in social work grew around him, all of them working in the nearby villages, and they included a Japanese monk. This ashram was named Sevagram and the Congress leaders had to travel there to meet Gandhiji, at times trudging through ankle-deep mud during the rains.

Bapu also decided that the Congress workers should experience village life first-hand. So the next annual session of the party in 1936 was held in Faizpur, a village in Maharashtra. The pandal was like a bamboo village designed by the famous artist from Shantiniketan, Nandalal Bose. Delegates were served village food, lived under thatched roofs and had to do all their sweeping and cleaning themselves. Bapu made sure that the Brahmins picked up the brooms. It was his way of introducing future ministers to their real constituents!

Critics of Gandhiji say he was against science and technology and wanted to go back to some ancient pre-industrial time, but that is not correct. He was just very suspicious of technology, and rightly so. What he did not like was our belief that any new technology is automatically good for us. Today when we take a look at our polluted rivers and our smog filled air, we know that he was perhaps correct. Industrialization has its adverse effects, and in most cases industries just make a few people very rich.

Often industries also deprive people of their livelihood. Take our tribal communities for example, who are losing their forests because of the mining industries, and this has spurred on the Naxal movement that is leading to so much violence. What Bapu wanted us to do is to judge every technology on its merits and decide whether we really need it or not. He wanted the people to decide, not the bureaucrat or politician. As he used to point out gently, even the charkha or a potter's wheel is a machine but it does not pollute, it does not take away people's livelihood but instead offers them a source of income.

He often spoke of turning 'waste into wealth' and was passionate about recycling things long before the word entered our vocabulary. He would use pencils until they were reduced to tiny stubs. He collected all the letters he received, and they came by the hundred every day. He opened out envelopes and used the blank sides of letters for his replies. Both his ashrams at Sabarmati and Sevagram were filled with trees, had kitchen gardens and there were cows and goats being tended by the children.

Gandhiji's ideal village was of a 'perfect democracy based on individual freedom' where the villagers would grow their own food, have a school, an auditorium and a medical clinic, good roads and shops. Everyone would find employment in the area and no one would be forced to migrate to the cities. Here elementary education would be free and children of all castes—both girls and boys— would study together. People called him a dreamer but in fact he was a supremely practical man devising practical solutions to poverty. And he was not afraid to fight for his dream.

8 🦌 The Lonely Pilgrim

1945–1948

The Second World War came to an end on 7 May 1945 when Germany surrendered to the Allied forces and Adolf Hitler died. Soon after, the United States dropped atom bombs on the cities of Hiroshima and Nagasaki, and Japan surrendered and withdrew from Burma. Then in the first British elections after the war Prime Minister Winston Churchill, the man who had led the Allies to victory, faced a shocking defeat. The new prime minister was Clement Attlee of the Labour Party, and unlike Churchill he was open to the idea of independence for India.

This radical change in the attitude of the British had come both because of the effects of many years of war and our freedom struggle. Both factors had made it impossible for Britain to hold on to the Indian empire. Fighting the war had left the British economy badly weakened; London had been bombed and many parts of the city had been turned into rubble. There were shortages of everything, from food items to clothing, and people were struggling to survive. At this time holding on to a rebellious empire was going to be a hard task. A whole generation of young men, who would have come to India as officers, had died on the battlefields and the army and bureaucracy in India was exhausted after the Quit India uprisings. Finally, after two centuries of colonial rule, the British were ready to go home.

There was also a big change in the attitude of Indians working in the government and the armed forces after the Quit India Movement. Many of them no longer felt any loyalty to the British, and also had a growing sense of confidence that they were ready to govern their own country without the presence of the British. There were sporadic strikes and even mutinies among sailors of the Royal Navy, who tore down the Union Jack and raised the tricolour on their ships in Bombay. The British decided to leave, not because of some generous wish to see a free India but because it could no longer hold on to the jewel of the British empire.

Negotiating for freedom

The fight to make the British leave had been a hard one, but the final struggle to create a united nation became much harder and much more complicated. Gandhiji left the job of negotiations to senior leaders like Jawaharlal Nehru, Maulana Azad, Sardar Patel and C. Rajagopalachari. He was always there to advise them, but as always he did not impose his wishes on anyone. These negotiations would finally lead to independence but only at the cost of dividing the country, something he had fought against all his life. At the end he had to agree with the other leaders that there was no other option, and it filled his heart with disappointment and sadness.

In March 1946 the British government sent the Cabinet Mission led by the Secretary of State Lord Pethick-Lawrence, and they faced an immensely complex political scene in India. It was not going to be a straightforward discussion between the government and the party that had fought for freedom, the Congress. Instead there were many parties claiming to represent different religions, communities and regions. There was the Muslim League, then the Hindu Mahasabha, the Sikh Akali Dal, B.R. Ambedkar representating the Dalits, and finally the most difficult bunch of all—the Indian princes. These were the rajas, maharajas and nawabs who had survived by being sycophant slaves of the British and they were now in panic, knowing full well that the Congress wanted a democratic government that had no place for kings. So they tried desperately to hold on to their kingdoms for as long as they could and opposed the Congress at every step.

The Cabinet Mission tried to please everyone and failed to win anyone's support. What they proposed was a country that would have provinces with democratic governments and princely states with monarchies. This would have created a nation that looked like a patchwork quilt as there were over 500 princely states strewn across India. This meant the princes would rule in their dictatorial way as before and the central democratic government would have no control over them. It was a recipe for disaster. The Cabinet Mission plan was immediately rejected by both the Congress and the Muslim League.

At the same time the Congress and the League, or rather Jinnah, were locked in a bitter battle. Jinnah declared that only his party represented the Muslims and dug his heels in and would not budge from his demand for Pakistan. This Two-Nation Theory went against everything Gandhiji had fought for, and he became deeply worried. He met Jinnah in Bombay for a series of talks, trying to make him change his mind. Jinnah imperiously refused to go and meet Gandhiji, so Bapu, who never had any problem with being courteous and co-operative, went to Jinnah's house for the meetings. For weeks the old man who lived in a village hut would patiently trudge up the marble staircase of Jinnah's palatial mansion in Bombay and try to convince him what a tragedy partition would be, but he failed.

Meanwhile, a national government was formed with a Constituent Assembly that would create the constitution for independent India. Nehru was the prime minister and headed the cabinet, which did not please the Muslim League. This was when Jinnah brought his threat of civil war out in the open. He declared 16 August 1946 as Direct Action Day to 'achieve Pakistan'. In Bengal, which had a League government, they deliberately started horrific communal riots. Muslims attacked Hindus and 5,000 people died in Calcutta. Then the conflagration spread when in retaliation Hindus began to attack Muslims in Bihar. An unrepentant Jinnah declared that 'India will be divided or destroyed' and the Congress feared that all of north India would be enveloped in the carnage. This would prove the British right when they said that Indians were not ready to govern themselves.

Walking alone

As the violence spread, Gandhiji ignored the advice of his colleagues and began to visit the places where the worst riots had taken place. He refused any police guards, and with just a few companions he walked through the countryside talking to people, desperately trying to establish peace. He went to the Bengal district of Noakhali and trudged from village to village, a seventy-seven-year-old man, unarmed and utterly vulnerable, heartbroken at the violence he saw all around him. He felt that somehow he had failed the people, and walked barefoot in penance across the rough village tracks, ignoring the cuts and bruises on his feet. He was never as courageous or as resolute and never as lonely. It was his finest hour as a humanitarian, and as B.R. Nanda writes, 'In the noble book of Gandhi's life this chapter is the noblest.'

In four months he covered 116 miles and visited forty-seven villages, often facing the anger of people who had lost everything, and he talked to them with endless patience, trying to convince them to end the violence. On his march to Dandi people had laid soft leaves under his feet. Now sometimes the paths were strewn with thorns and broken glass. When he entered a village he would go to the hut of a Muslim and ask for shelter and at times the door would be slammed on his face. He sat and listened to endless stories of personal tragedies, of lives lost, lives ruined. He slept wherever he could, eating whatever they gave him, and moved on the next day.

The warrior of peace was on another lonely journey, in an echo of his favourite Tagore song *Ekla chalo*.

There had been trouble between Hindus and Muslims before, but they were always provoked by local disputes and always died down quickly. It was Jinnah who turned communal violence into a political weapon, where his men would start riots as a political threat. With the violence in Bengal he showed the Congress that he did not have the slightest regret at the massacre of innocent people as long as he got what he wanted. He was the complete opposite of Gandhiji, who said that religion was a personal matter and should never be part of the political life of a nation and that non-violence was essential for any political struggle.

Jinnah made religion the core of his demands, insisting Muslims belonged to a separate nation when in fact people were really separated by differences in their regions and languages. For example, a Bengali Muslim had nothing in common with a Muslim in Punjab but shared a common culture with Bengali Hindus. Jinnah made religion a political issue, encouraged a spirit of intolerance among Muslims, as if it was something they should be proud of, and ultimately created an Islamic state. What he never understood was something Gandhiji had always said, that both violence and intolerance always spiral out of control and never end. One day it is Hindus against Muslims, next it is Shias against Sunnis, and violence starts the fires of revenge that are very hard to quench. Jinnah never understood that politics of hate and intolerance does not build nations.

While Gandhiji was far away in Bengal and Bihar, in Delhi the Congress leaders finally bowed before the threat of a civil war and agreed to a division of the country. When the Congress Working Committee voted for the partition of India, Gandhiji finally lost all hope and from then on he left all political work to the others and went back to his struggle for peace. He wanted no hand in the division of his motherland. At one time he used to say humorously that he had so much work to do that he would like to live to the age of 125, but not any more.

Lord Louis Mountbatten arrived as India's last viceroy to supervise the partition of the country. He decided that India would become independent on 15 August 1947. The new nation of Pakistan would include the areas with a Muslim majority—Baluchistan, Sindh, North-West Frontier Province, West Punjab and East Bengal. So it would be a country with provinces at two ends of the subcontinent. Jinnah, who had grandiosely claimed all of Punjab, Bengal and also Kashmir and Assam, was of course furious and complained bitterly at the 'moth-eaten' Pakistan that had been created.

One people, two nations

The Congress had hoped that partition would stop the communal carnage, but what followed was a human tragedy no one could have imagined. Hindus fled Pakistan, Muslims left India and soon twenty million people had crossed the borders and the violence raged in cities and villages. No one has an exact number, but historians estimate that close to a million people lost their lives and the rest were homeless, penniless, traumatized and angry refugees. Interestingly, even then a large section of Muslims refused to listen to Jinnah's call and chose to remain in India and they proved him wrong when he claimed to represent all Muslims.

At midnight on 15 August 1947, Jawaharlal Nehru was sworn in as the first prime minister of India. It was a glittering ceremony in the central hall of parliament, with Mountbatten in a medal-encrusted uniform and his wife in a gorgeous ball gown and wearing a tiara, sitting on thrones. As a host of dignitaries and Congress leaders watched and Indians stayed awake to listen to him on the radio, Nehru, the poet-balladeer, raised his voice and began, 'Long years ago we made a tryst with destiny, and now the time comes when we shall redeem our pledge, not wholly or in full measure, but very substantially. At the stroke of midnight hour, when the world sleeps, India shall awake to life and freedom . . .'

One man was missing from the gathering, the man who had done the most to achieve this moment; who had spent a lifetime dreaming of such a day, but at the end his dream of a many-hued rainbow nation had been shattered, and he was not going to celebrate it. Gandhiji was far away from Delhi, quietly helping the people of Calcutta. He was staying in the home of a Muslim, and spent the day fasting and praying. As crowds celebrated in the streets of India, waving flags and bursting crackers, one wonders if anyone had the courage to go up to him and ask what he felt.

In Calcutta he had gone on a fast till the rioting stopped and his presence in Bengal led to the region staying comparatively peaceful during the exodus of the population. At the same time army regiments were struggling to establish peace in Punjab and Sind. Mountbatten watched the moral authority of this one frail man with amazement and sent a telegram to Gandhiji that said, 'My dear Gandhiji, in the Punjab we have 55,000 soldiers and large-scale rioting on our hands. In Bengal our forces consist of one man and there is no rioting. As a serving officer, as well as an administrator, may I be allowed to pay my tribute to the One Man Boundary Force . . .'

Things were going out of control in Delhi, where thousands of refugees had arrived, and Muslims faced their rage. In desperation Nehru begged Gandhiji to come. When he arrived he went on another fast that nearly killed him, but it did restore peace. He was exhausted but continued to work long hours visiting troubled areas, talking to people, conferring with leaders and arranging help for the refugees. He went from one refugee camp to another without any police escort and commented sadly that it seemed everyone was angry with him. He knew his work was not done and was planning to leave for Punjab and was even thinking of visiting Pakistan.

Usually Bapu stayed at a sweeper's colony in Delhi, but as it was filled with refugees he was staying at Birla

House. Here, hundreds of people would gather in the mornings and evenings for his prayer meetings. There was great resentment among Hindu communal parties because they felt that Gandhiji was favouring the Muslims. On 20 January 1948, a bomb was thrown into his prayer meeting but fortunately he was not hurt. Ignoring the disturbance he calmly went on speaking and later when Sardar Patel wanted to tighten the security he refused to let the police search the people.

On the evening of 30 January, Gandhiji, who was a stickler for punctuality, was hurrying towards the prayer meeting as he was a few minutes late. He left his room leaning on his two 'walking sticks'—his grand nieces Abha and Manu—and headed towards the garden. A man wearing khaki-coloured clothes broke through the surging crowds and bent down as if to touch his feet. Gandhiji raised his hand to bless him. Manu tried to make the man move away, but he pushed past her and then raised a revolver and shot at Gandhiji thrice. As he fell to the ground, his shawl staining red, Bapu breathed softly, 'Hey Ram!'

The warrior for peace had given his life to his lifelong quest. The assassin was a Hindu bigot and a RSS sympathizer, who thought he was killing a man who favoured Muslims over Hindus. In fact, what Nathuram Godse did was silence the voice that could have taught India to live in religious harmony in the future. India fell silent in shock and grief. No one could get over the thought that this man of peace, who had been a father to his people, could be killed by his own countryman.

And as B.R. Nanda writes thoughtfully, 'In death he achieved what he had tried so hard in his last days to achieve, the return of sanity to the Indo–Pakistan sub–continent.'

The announcement of Gandhiji's passing away was made on the radio by Jawaharlal Nehru who said in a shaking voice, 'The light has gone out of our lives and there is darkness everywhere and I do not quite know what to tell you and how to say it. Our beloved leader, Bapu as we call him, the father of our nation, is no more . . . The light has gone out, I said, and yet I was wrong. For the light that shone in this country was no ordinary light. The light that has illumined the country for these many years will illumine this country for many more years, and a thousand years later that light will still be seen in the country, and the world will see it and it will give solace to innumerable hearts.'

Six decades after he left us, the world has still not forgotten Mohandas Karamchand Gandhi, the man of truth, love, non–violence and peace.

Making friends

Mahatma Gandhi made friends wherever he went. A successful South African architect, the daughter of a British rear admiral and an English priest were among the many foreigners who became close friends and loyal associates of Gandhiji.

Charles Freer Andrews (1871–1940) studied at Cambridge and was then ordained in the Church of England as a priest. He came to India in 1904 to teach philosophy at St. Stephens College in Delhi and soon began a campaign to elect an Indian principal for the college. He was so popular with his students that they named him Deenabandhu—friend of the poor. At a public meeting at Lahore he heard about Gandhiji's satyagraha in South Africa and immediately donated all his savings to the cause. The Congress leader G.K. Gokhale then sent Andrews to South Africa to convince Gandhiji to return to India.

The two men took to each other immediately and a close friendship began that lasted for the rest of their lives. Andrews was the only person who called Gandhiji 'Mohan' and he was 'Dearest Charlie' in the letters Bapu wrote to him. Gandhiji used the initials of Andrews' name and came up with a new title—'Christ's Faithful Apostle'. He also called him the 'Good Samaritan'. All the names reflect the innate goodness and generosity of the man.

Andrews often spoke publicly and wrote in newspapers in favour of Indian independence. In South Africa he helped Gandhiji edit the journal *Indian Opinion*, while in India he often acted as a liaison between him and the government. He was also part of the entourage to London in 1931 for the Round Table Conference. He was involved in many social causes like the rights of Indian indentured labourers in Fiji, and worked with B.R. Ambedkar in his fight against untouchability.

Andrews spent many years in Shantiniketan, poet Rabindranath Tagore's ashram school, and there is a hazy black-and-white photograph of him, Gandhiji and Tagore sitting together and chatting like old friends. Like Tagore he did not always agree with Gandhiji and was always ready to tell him so. During the First World War when Gandhiji supported the British and even started a volunteer force, Andrews did not approve. He also disliked Gandhiji's fasts even though he nursed his friend through one. In one letter he wrote, 'Only with the greatest difficulty that I find myself able to justify it under any circumstance.'

In 1935 Gandhiji requested Andrews to move away from the freedom movement as he felt that the campaign should be led only by Indians. Though disappointed, Andrews agreed and became more involved with social work, but the two of them carried on a voluminous correspondence, with Gandhiji sending him detailed reports. C.F. Andrews died in Calcutta in 1940 without seeing his dream of a free India.

Hermann Kallenbach (1871–1945) was one of the earliest supporters of Gandhiji in South Africa along with Bapu's secretary Sonya Schlesin and the journalist H.S.L. Polak. Kallenbach was a successful architect who was deeply influenced by the philosophy of ahimsa. A bachelor and a rich man, he donated 1,000 acres of land about twenty miles from Johannesburg to Gandhiji. Here the commune Tolstoy Farm came up. Soon Kallenbach had joined the farm and become a vegetarian. He built the corrugated roof huts for the inmates, ran a school for children and did all the carpentry work. He learnt to make shoes from German monks and also taught Bapu.

Kallenbach was a boxer and a wrestler, but his belief in ahimsa was so strong that he refused a challenge to a duel by a white man critical of Gandhiji. During their trial after the satyagraha, Kallenbach, Gandhiji and Polak were determined to go to prison so they obligingly gave evidence against each other! He visited India twice and stayed at the Sewagram Ashram in Wardha.

Kallenbach was a Jew and disagreed with Gandhiji's pacifist suggestion that everyone should pray for Hitler to change and use non-violent methods to fight the Nazis. A practical man, Kallenbach knew well that there were times when one had to take up arms against great evil and injustice. He was a supporter of Zionism and left all his money for the future state of Israel.

We know her as **Mira Behn** but she was born Madeleine Slade (1892–1982), the daughter of a British rear admiral. She was a musician and also interested in philosophy and became fascinated by the idea of satyagraha and ahimsa. She had little money, and sold a brooch for twenty pounds and sent the money to Gandhiji. In turn he invited her to come to Sabarmati Ashram in 1925.

Slade was deeply impressed by Gandhiji and decided to remain in India. She learnt Hindi, cut off her hair, wore a white sari and lived the simple life of the ashram, spinning and doing all the daily chores. Her devotion to Gandhiji was absolute and he treated her like a daughter. He named her Mira Behn after the Bhakti poet Mira Bai.

In the beginning she did not find life in India easy, especially the climate, but she never gave up. Soon she was acting as a secretary to Gandhiji and helped to translate his autobiography *My Experiments with Truth*. Like C.F. Andrews she often became Bapu's personal emissary to the viceroy and took care of him during his travels. She was always very particular that he ate his meals on time and once walked into a meeting between the viceroy Lord Mountbatten and Gandhiji at Viceregal Lodge (Rashtrapati Bhawan), carrying his wooden bowl of dates and milk.

Mira Behn was also part of the entourage to London for the Round Table Conference. She joined the Civil Disobedience Movement, was arrested and sent to Arthur Road jail, where she was put in a prison cell with criminals. She later wrote a detailed report about the conditions inside the prison and the way freedom fighters were treated. During the Quit India Movement she was again arrested and sent to the Aga Khan Palace with Bapu and Kasturba. Here she took care of Kasturba when she fell ill and later died.

Mira Behn started an ashram near Roorkee in Uttar Pradesh in 1942. She left for England in 1959 and later lived in Vienna. At the invitation of Lord Mounbatten she came to London in 1969 to join the centenary celebrations of Gandhiji's birth and spoke to a huge gathering at the Royal Albert Hall. She was awarded the Padma Vibhushan in 1981 and died a year later at the age of ninety.

We remember Gandhiji's Indian associates like Sardar Patel, Jawaharlal Nehru, Sarojini Naidu and Maulana Azad, but sadly memories of C.F. Andrews, Hermann Kallenbach and Mira Behn have faded from public memory. They may not have been Indians, but they were true satyagrahis and freedom fighters.

TRIVIA
TREASURY

Turn the pages to discover more fascinating facts and tantalizing tidbits of history about this legendary life and his world.

WHAT HAPPENED AND WHEN

- **1869, 2 October:** Mohandas Karamchand Gandhi was born in Porbandar, Gujarat.
- **1882:** Gandhiji is married to Kasturba Makhanji.
- **1891:** He gets a law degree in London.
- **1893:** He sails for Durban, South Africa.
- **1904:** He founds Phoenix Farm at Durban.
- **1907:** The first satyagraha takes place at Transvaal, South Africa.
- **1910:** Gandhiji founds Tolstoy Farm near Johannesburg.
- **1914:** He returns to India, travels across the country.
- **1917:** Establishes the Sabarmati Ashram in Ahmedabad.
- **1917:** The Champaran satyagraha campaign takes place.
- **1919:** Gandhiji starts a hartal against the Rowlatt Act.
- **1920:** He launches the Non-cooperation Movement.
- **1928:** The Bardoli satyagraha campaign takes place.
- **1930:** He starts the Civil Disobedience Movement with the Dandi March.
- **1931:** Gandhi–Irwin talks take place.
- **1931:** He attends the Round Table Conference in London.
- **1933:** Establishes Sewagram Ashram at Wardha.

- **1942:** Launches the Quit India agitation in Bombay.
- **1942:** He is arrested and imprisoned with Kasturba.
- **1942:** Mahadev Desai dies in prison.
- **1944:** Kasturba dies in prison.
- **1944:** He talks with Jinnah to avoid a partition of India.
- **1946:** Travels to Bengal to establish peace after the communal riots.
- **1947:** Fasts to restore communal harmony.
- **1947, 15 August:** As India becomes independent, Gandhiji is in Calcutta doing social work post the partition of India.
- **1948, 30 January:** He is assassinated by Nathuram Godse while on his way to a prayer meeting in Delhi

AS BAPU SAID . . .

On Ahimsa

- Ahimsa is the highest ideal. It is meant for the brave, never for the cowardly.
- An eye for an eye makes the whole world blind.
- Ahimsa is an attribute of the brave. Cowardice and ahimsa don't go together any more than water and fire.
- My ahimsa would not tolerate the idea of giving a free meal to a healthy person who has not worked for it in some honest way.

On Satyagraha

- Satyagraha has been designed as an effective substitute for violence and war.
- A satyagrahi has infinite patience, abundant faith in others and ample hope.
- In the code of the satyagrahi, there is no such thing as surrender to brute force.
- A satyagrahi enjoys a degree of freedom not possible for others, for he becomes a truly fearless person. Once his mind is rid of fear, he will never agree to be another's slave.

WHAT THE WORLD SAID ABOUT BAPU . . .

'Generations to come will scarce believe that such a one as this ever in flesh and blood walked upon this earth.'

—Albert Einstein, scientist

'He was one who could combine kranti (revolution) with shanti (peace).'

—Vinobha Bhave, social activist

'Gandhi fell with a railway ticket no one honoured, he rose with a testament none could ignore; he fell a passenger but rose a patriot; he fell a barrister but rose a revolutionary.'

—G.K. Gokhale, Congress leader

'Christ gave us the goals and Mahatma Gandhi, the tactics.'
            —Martin Luther King Jr, civil rights activist

A humorous poem by a man who knew him best—
Mahadev Desai who was his secretary and constant
companion for many years:
    To live with the saints in heaven,
    Is a bliss and a glory.
    But to live with a saint on earth,
    Is a different story.

Finally Bapu on himself:
'Men say I am a saint losing myself in politics. The fact is
that I am a politician trying my hardest to be a saint.'

MUSEUMS AND MEMORIALS TO VISIT

Even today people go by the thousands to Raj Ghat and
Birla House in Delhi to pay their respects to Gandhiji.
He was killed at Birla House and his funeral was held at
Raj Ghat in 1948. Across the road from Raj Ghat is the
Gandhi Smarak Nidhi Museum that has many fascinating
photographs, including one of him riding a bicycle and
another of him wearing a huge Assamese hat! All the
things he used, like clothes, walking stick, chappals and
his round framed glasses, are displayed here. One room

displays hundreds of stamps from across the world with his face on them. You can buy books on Bapu here.

In Ahmedabad, Gujarat, the Sabarmati Ashram still thrives. It is a peaceful, serene place, and you will sense that Bapu's spirit is still there as you wander around the red tiled huts and under shady trees. Also, many of the places he visited or stayed at have small memorials built in his honour, like at Dandi and at the Aga Khan Palace near Pune.

FASCINATING FACTS ABOUT BAPU

- His favourite songs included *Vaishnava jana to*, a bhajan composed by Narsingh Mehta, *Ekla chalo* by Rabindranath Tagore; the bhajan *Raghupati raghav* and the hymns *Abide with me* and *Lead kindly light*.
- Every January, during the Beating the Retreat ceremony after the Republic Day celebrations, the last tune that is always played is *Abide with me*.
- His ashes were put in brass urns and some were immersed in the Ganga. One urn was found in a bank vault in 1997 and the ashes taken to Allahabad for immersion by his family. Another was discovered in South Africa in 2010 and immersed in the ocean there.
- He edited a number of journals—*Harijan, Indian Opinion, Young India*.
- The greatest apostle for peace never won the Nobel

Peace Prize! He was nominated five times. He was to get it in 1948, but unfortunately he died the same year. That year no prize was awarded.

- He was elected president of the Indian National Congress only once—in 1924 at Belgaum.
- The largest biographies of Bapu are the eight volumes by D.G. Tendulkar and the ten volumes by his secretary Pyarelal.
- Richard Attenborough directed the film *Gandhi* in 1982. The role of Bapu was played by Ben Kingsley. It won eight Academy Awards, including Best Film and Best Actor.
- A number of other films have been made on Bapu's life or he has appeared in them. These are *Gandhi, My Father* (2007), *The Making of a Mahatma* (1996) and *Lage Raho Munnabhai* (2006), which coined the word *gandhigiri*.

CHILDREN OF GANDHI

Time magazine listed leaders who are Bapu's spiritual heirs, calling them 'Children of Gandhi'. In the years after Bapu's death, these men and women have fought for equality and freedom through peaceful means and proved that non-violent movements can succeed.

These international satyagrahis are—the Dalai Lama of Tibet; Martin Luther King Jr of the United States;

Desmond Tutu and Nelson Mandela of South Africa; Aung San Suu Kyi of Myanmar; Lech Walesa of Poland; Benigno Aquino Jr of the Philippines; and Cesar Chavez, an American labour leader.

Their lives show how difficult and challenging satyagraha can be. King and Aquino were assassinated. Mandela and Suu Kyi faced long imprisonments and the latter has been under house arrest for over twenty years. The Dalai Lama has been in exile from his homeland for over five decades. At the same time, the African Americans have won equality through the efforts of Martin Luther King Jr. Desmond Tutu and Nelson Mandela have ended apartheid in South Africa, and democracy has been established in the Philippines and Poland. Satyagraha has won.

BOOKS TO READ

Here are some books you can read if you want to know more about Gandhiji and India's freedom struggle.

1. *The Life of Mahatma Gandhi* by Louis Fischer (Harper Collins, 1951)
2. *Mahatma Gandhi: A Biography* by B.R. Nanda (Oxford University Press, 1958)
3. *Gandhi: Prisoner of Hope* by Judith M. Brown (Oxford University Press, 1989)

4. *Gandhi: A Life Re-visited* by Krishna Kripalani (Mehta Publishers, 1983)
5. *Mahatma Gandhi: Apostle of Non-violence* by Coonoor Kripalani (Rupa, 2003)
6. *India's Struggle for Independence* by Bipan Chandra and others (Penguin, 1988)
7. *The Making of a Nation* by B.R. Nanda (Harper Collins, 1998)
8. *Struggle for Freedom* edited by R.C. Majumdar (Bharatiya Vidya Bhavan, 1969)
9. *A Flag, a Song and a Pinch of Salt: Freedom Fighters of India* by Subhadra Sen Gupta (Puffin, 2007)
10. *Saffron, White & Green: The Amazing Story of India's Independence* by Subhadra Sen Gupta (Puffin, 2008)

You can also search on the Internet. There are many websites that have the life of Gandhiji and also lots of photographs. Check out www.mkgandhi.org and www.saltmarch.org. On www.wikipedia.org. there is a large entry on Gandhi and also on other freedom fighters. And if you want to read more, just Google!

If you have any questions about the freedom movement you can always mail me at subhadrasg@gmail.com.

Other Books in the Series

Ashoka: The Great and Compassionate King
By Subhadra Sen Gupta

After the fierce battle of Kalinga, the victorious king stood in the middle of the terrible carnage he had wrought, in a battlefield filled with the dead and dying, and took a close look at what he had achieved . . .

The transformation that came over this king after one of his most significant victories at war made him into a legend forever. Ashoka the Great, the ruler of ancient India's largest kingdom, took the path of peace, tolerance, non-violence and compassion. He now addressed his subjects as a father would his children, and erected pillars that spread his thoughts throughout the land in the people's own language. He put their welfare above all else and worked towards that for the rest of his life. One of the most well-known symbols from India's history, the Ashoka chakra, now adorns India's national flag, and the lion capital from his pillars is our national emblem.

In this lively, engrossing account of Ashoka's life and the times, Subhadra Sen Gupta deftly brings him alive again from behind the swirling mists of time. It is a story about war, devotion and a king's love for his people, embellished with many details about Mauryan society, battle codes and even freaky food facts! Plunge into some of the most dramatic episodes of India's history with the *Puffin Lives* series and let the past speak to you like never before.

Other Books in the Series

Jawaharlal Nehru: The Jewel of India
By Aditi De

At midnight on 14 August 1947, Jawaharlal Nehru rose to speak to independent India as its first Prime Minister. He was dressed in a pale cream *achkan,* a white khadi cap on his head. Though his eyes had shadows beneath them, they grew brighter as Jawaharlal began to speak . . .

Pandit Nehru's words that night have remained etched in the nation's memory ever since. Born to a privileged family in Allahabad, Jawaharlal went on to become a leading figure of the Indian independence movement. During the struggle he spent over ten years in prison, watched others in his family jailed time and again, and led numerous protest marches and agitations. Working alongside Mahatma Gandhi, he helped India keep its tryst with destiny and become a free nation.

Aditi De recounts the story of Jawaharlal Nehru's extraordinary life in this sparkling biography for young readers. Filled with charming anecdotes, it recounts episodes from Nehru's childhood, and how he was drawn to the growing struggle for Indian independence. She sketches his role as the first Indian Prime Minister, and how he shaped the newly-formed democratic republic. Packed with little-known nuggets of information, and trivia about the times, this book in the *Puffin Lives* series brings alive the thoughts and actions of one of modern India's most important personalities.

Other Books in the Series

Rani Lakshmibai: The Valiant Queen of Jhansi
By Deepa Agarwal

The elephant obediently sank on its knees, responding to its mahout's commands. Three men mounted it. A little girl came running up. 'Wait, I want to ride it too! I want to ride it too!' she clamoured. The men ignored her pointedly. Her father Moropant pulled her away. 'It's not in your destiny to ride elephants,' he said.

The girl's large eyes flashed. 'It's my destiny to ride ten. Wait and see, Baba!'

A little girl Manikarnika, with an uncanny sense of her own destiny, grew up to be none other than the brave queen of Jhansi, Rani Lakshmibai. Trained in horse riding and the martial arts from an early age, Manu was married to Gangadhar Rao, the Maharaja of Jhansi, when she was thirteen. Soon after her husband's death, the reins of the kingdom passed on to her, and she took up this responsibility undeterred and fearless. When Jhansi faced the danger of annexation, she fought against the British with unflinching courage, losing her life in the course of the battle. She has since become one of the most inspiring heroes of the freedom struggle and a much-admired role model.

Deepa Agarwal chronicles the life and times of this legendary character in a gripping narrative, drawing a colourful portrait of bravery. This riveting account also includes nuggets of information about the eventful year 1857, making for a fascinating read.

Other Books in the Series

Akbar: The Mighty Emperor
By Kavitha Mandana

The birth of a prince in medieval India was usually followed by grand celebrations. Akbar's birth certainly lifted the flagging spirits of the Mughals. But the celebrations were muted. Camped out in the wilderness when the news of Akbar's safe delivery reached him, Humayun could only enjoy a quiet moment of thanksgiving. He broke a musk pod and, as the fragrance wafted all over the camp, the new father hoped his son's fame would similarly spread across the world.

Akbar—emperor, warrior, statesman and thinker—is acknowledged as one of the most charismatic personalities in Indian history. Crowned the king of Hindustan at the age of thirteen, his empire expanded to include the farthest corners of the country. Yet he was not just a conqueror. A humanist, Akbar's deep interest in literature, architecture, art, and his inclusive vision of religions at a time when such thoughts were not in fashion, set him down as one of history's most remarkable men.

In this story of his life, as exciting and thrilling as any adventure tale, the author describes Akbar's rough, difficult childhood spent on the run; his consolidation of the empire through war and diplomacy; the myriad interesting and entertaining people who made up his court; the strong women of the Mughal household; and, finally, the intriguing circumstances under which the crown passed on to his son, Jehangir. Accompanied by many interesting facts about the Mughal empire and the world in the 16th century, this book is a fascinating introduction to the life and times of an emperor who still rules our imaginations.